REMEMBERING

(Korea: 1950-1953)

by

Dennis J Ottley

RoseDog Books
PITTSBURGH, PENNSYLVANIA 15238

RoseDog Books
585 Alpha Drive
Suite 103
Pittsburgh, PA 15238
Visit our website at *www.rosedogbookstore.com*

ISBN: 978-1-4809-6179-1
eISBN: 978-1-4809-6156-2

CONTENTS

SFC Dennis J. Ottley

The above sketch was drawn by a Japanese artist while standing on a street corner in downtown Tokyo, Japan – April 1952

DEDICATION

I dedicate this story to one of my best friends, Paul Norman Oaks, who was killed in action during the Korean War on November 9, 1950. Paul's home town was Vernal, Uintah County, UT. My family had resided in Vernal from 1945 through 1947. During this time, Paul and I attended Uintah High School together and got to be the best of friends. After my family and I left Vernal in December of 1947, Paul and I kept in close touch with each other up until the time of his death.

Paul and I were both born on January 28, 1932. Some people might have thought we were brothers, maybe even twin brothers. We both turned 18 years old on January 28, 1950, and shortly after that Paul joined the United States Army. I probably would have joined with him, but at that time, my wife, Sandy, and I were planning to be married in July.

After Paul had joined the army, he received his training at Fort Benning, GA, and Fort Ord, CA, before going overseas with an airborne division. Paul had certified for the paratroopers and had received his wings.

On June 25, 1950, the North Koreans crossed the 38th Parallel, attacking South Korea; this started the war between the two countries known as the Korean War. On July 14, Paul was on his way for duty in Korea.

Therefore, I dedicate this book to PFC Paul Norman Oaks, killed in action.
And
In memory of all Korean War Veterans who made the supreme sacrifice
as they fought for freedom...

Paul Norman Oaks, PFC was a member of E (Easy) Company of the 38th Infantry Regiment, 2nd Infantry Division. He was seriously wounded by the enemy in South Korea on September 1, 1950. He had been hit four times. He was hit in the left elbow, the left side of his chest, his left shoulder, which fractured his collar bone, and in the back of his head; he was taken to Osaka, Japan, and hospitalized in the Osaka General Hospital. While in the hospital, he wrote me a letter on September 8, 1950, his last letter to me. Weeks later I answered his letter, but apparently I hadn't answered it soon enough, because my letter was returned marked "VERIFIED DECEASED." Apparently, after Paul was released from the hospital in Osaka on October 27, 1950, he had returned to front-line duty in Korea. A couple of weeks later, he was killed in action while fighting the enemy near Tuom-ni in North Korea on November 9, 1950.

Why Paul returned to duty in Korea after being so seriously wounded on September 1, 1950, I will never know. A soldier being wounded that badly would normally get his ticket home, but knowing Paul as I did, I would bet that it was his choice to return to the battlefield.

Paul's body was not returned to his home in Vernal, UT, until January of 1955. At that time, his mother planned a funeral for him and called me to be a pall bearer. I accepted and felt extremely honored that she would remember me enough to ask me. He was a good friend and a great guy.

Sept. 8, 1950
Osaka, Japan

Dear Dennis
Well I thought I would
write and see how you was
doing. Did you get my last
letter ok. I didn't no your
address but I thought that
was it. Well it has been
quite awhile since I have
saw you, are you married yet.

I guess your wondering
what I am doing in Japan,
well it started early one
morning in Korea, they att-
acted us and I got hit four
times al up along the left

side, the first was in my
left elbow, left chest, Left
shoulder, which fractured
the collor bone, and the
last one in the rear of
my head, and know I set
and lay in the Osaka Gen-
ereal Hosipital, and that
is a pretty good story of it.
It is really rough in Korerea
know, all we need is more
men, but you know they
just can't get over here fast
enough. You know Korerea
reminded me quite a bit

of Wyoming and Montana it
is very rockie, and I think
all of it is mountains
because I really got tired
of fighting in them. I don't
know weather I'll get to come
to the states or what, a captain told me here that I
should get to come to the states
on this fractured shoulder, I
hope so".

Well kid what have you
been doing for yourself lately.
Have you heard from Joe lately
or has he been writing to you.

- over

Oh before I forget tell your mother and the rest of them hello, and I hope they are all feeling well. Is Kent and his wife still around there, also Benjamin Johnny, where are they. Well I am starting to pain a little bit so I better be closing for know, so answer soon won't you.

Your Pal

Paul

"The tree of liberty must be refreshed from time to time with the blood of patriots and tyrants." —Thomas Jefferson

Pvt. Paul Norman Oaks . . .
Claims he was only one left alive.

Vernal Soldier Wounded in Korean War

VERNAL (Special)—Pvt. Paul Norman Oaks, 18, son of Mrs. Rulon Cook, Vernal, was wounded in action in Korea Sept. 1, according to word received from the army department, Sept. 15.

In a letter to his mother, Pvt. Oaks said that he had received head wounds, a fractured left shoulder and elbow and chest wounds. He is now recovering in a hospital in Japan. He also said that he was the only one of his unit to escape alive.

He enlisted Feb. 1, 1950, after attending Uintah high school, receiving his training at Fort Benning, Ga., and Fort Ord, Cal., before going overseas with an airborne division.

Paul N. Oaks

VERNAL — Funeral services for Pfc. Paul Norman Oaks, who was killed in action in Korea Nov. 9, 1950, will be held Thursday at 1 p.m. in the Vernal Second Ward Chapel, Church of Jesus Christ of Latter-day Saints.

Friends may call at the home of a brother Martin E. Oaks, 186 East 1st South, Thursday morning from 10 a.m. until service time. Burial will

Pfc. Oaks

be in the Maeser Fairview Cemetery, with military rites by the American Legion Witbeck Post No. 11. Pfc. Oaks was born Jan. 28, 1932, in Vernal, a son of James Edwin and Marell Nelson Oaks. He attended Uintah High School before enlisting in the Army Feb. 1, 1950.

PFC PAUL N OAKS

38th Infantry Regiment
E CO

2nd Infantry Division

Army

Hostile, Died (KIA)

Date Of Loss: November 9, 1950

Service Number: RA19343957

UINTAH COUNTY, UT

Location of Loss: TUOM-NI

Year of Birth: 1932

Comments: Private First Class Oaks was a member of the
38th Infantry Regiment, 2nd Infantry Division. He was
seriously wounded by the enemy in South Korea on
September 1, 1950 and returned to duty on October 27,
1950. He was Killed in Action while fighting the enemy in
North Korea on November 9, 1950.

Korean War Project Key No: 22125

*Poster from the Korean War Memorial in Washington D.C. describing Paul Oak's
unit and date of death…*

Thank You.

Remembering
Korea: 1950-1953

About the Author:

If you have ever met Dennis Ottley, you will hear his voice in every line of this account of his life from 1950-1952. This book follows an 18 year-old boy form his hometown in WY to a world thousands of miles away to fight for a cause he was almost too young to understand at the time. "Remembering" is just that. Dennis recalls with amazing clarity the events, the experiences, the people, the weather and even the "chow" for the nearly 2 years he spent away from everything familiar to him.

He tells the story in print just as he has told the stories for years to his children, his grandchildren and even his great-grandchildren; not with a boastful air of bravado, not with an emphasis on the gore or the devastation or the emotional toll of war, but with the simple humility that has graced all the pages of Dennis' life. He may have marched off to Korea as a boy, but he came home as a man characterized with discipline, honor, integrity and a pride for his country and for service to it. May we never forget to be grateful for those who serve.

Written by: Kerri Reeves Ottley
Daughter-in-law

ACKNOWLEDGMENTS

I, the author, wish to thank my wife, Sandy, for her encouragement, her suggestions, and for her willingness to edit the story. In addition, I would like to mention and thank Paul Vosakis, an Evanston High School classmate, an Army buddy, and a lifetime good friend for his help in recalling some of the happenings. Plus, I wish to show my appreciation to my business assistant, Maryl Thompson, for her knowledge and assistance on helping me operate the computer.

AND a special thanks to the following authors and publishers for permission to use materials and information from their books and publications:

Excerpt from THE KOREAN WAR: Pusan To Chosin, An Oral History by Donald Know. Copyright 1985 by Donald Know. Reprinted by permission of Houghton Mifflin Harcourt Publishing Company. All rights reserved.

Copyright: 2000, Potomac Books/An Imprint of the University of Nebraska Press, Dulles VA; THE KOREAN WAR: The Story and the Photographs, by Donald M. Goldstein and Harry J. Maihafer.

The *Twenty-First Infantry Division: Tropic Lightning*, Korea 1950-1954 by John Keliher Morgan and Randy Baumgardner, edited by Sincock 2002 Turner Publishing Company. ALL RIGHTS RESERVED.

THE COLDEST WINTER: America and the Korean War (New York: Hyperion), 2007 by David Halberstam, author and Little, Brown and Company as publisher.

KOREAN WAR ALMANAC, 1990 by Harry G. Summers, Colonel of Infantry, U.S. Armu (Ret.), published by Facts On File, Inc.

The Korean War Veterans Association's official publication of "THE GRAYBEARDS", published by Finisterre Publishing Company.

The Veterans of Foreign War's issue of THE BATTLES OF THE KOREAN WAR, Americans Engage in Deadly Combat, 1950-1953 and Richard Kolb, Editor-in-Chief.

In expressing my thanks to those parties named above, the conclusions and errors this book may contain are the full responsibility of myself

Dennis J. Ottley, Author
Evanston, Wyoming

Thoughts From "Over There" – A Soldier's Poem
By Edwin Laub, 1932

I'm sitting here and thinking of the things I left behind,

And I'd hate to put on paper what is running through my mind.

We've dug a million ditches and cleared ten miles of ground,

And a meaner place this side of Hell is waiting to be found.

But there is one consolation – gather closely while I tell.

When we die we'll go to Heaven, for we've done our hitch in Hell!

We've built a hundred kitchens for the cooks to stew our beans.

We've stood a million guard-mounts and cleaned the camp's latrine.

We've washed a million mess-kits and peeled a million spuds.

We've rolled a million blanket rolls and washed our Captain's duds.

The number of parades we've stood is very hard to sell.

We won't have to parade in Heaven for we've done our hitch in Hell!

We've killed a million rats and bugs that cried out for our eats,

And shook a million centipedes out of our dirty sheets.

We've marched a million miles and made a million camps,

And have pulled a million cactus' from the seat of khaki pants.

But, when our work on earth is done, our friends behind will tell —

"When they died they went to Heaven," for they'd done their hitch in Hell.

When finally taps is sounded and we lay aside life's care,

We will do our last parade up those shining Golden-Stairs.

The angels all will welcome us and harps will start to play,

We will draw a million canteen bucks and spend them in a day.

It is then we'll hear St. Peter tell us loudly with a yell,

"Take a front seat, boys, for you've done your hitch in Hell."

INTRODUCTION

KOREA: 1950-1953…a war that some called the "FORGOTTEN WAR." Statesman Averell Harriman said it was "a sour little war." However, thousands of men and women who served in Korea during that time would differ. These people served in many different capacities, but all remember the heartaches, the deaths, the wounded, and the mass destruction caused during this period. We all remember the hot summers and the freezing cold winters. Forgotten? No way, to us the Korean War had never been forgotten.

This was a war that President Harry S. Truman proclaimed to be nothing but "a police action" and entered the conflict without a declaration of war. It was years before Congress ever acknowledged it as a full scale war. Pres. Truman tried to persuade a reluctant United Nations into participating in the war with the United States, but only 15 nations plus the USA agreed to participate on the side of the South at the start. Russia and China supported the North; Russia with weapons and equipment, and China with troops.

President Truman believed that the Soviet Union (Russia) and Communist China conspired to start the war. At the time of the invasion, communism assumed that Korea would be the first step toward a plan for world conquest. However, some historians believed that America instigated the war, using South Koreans as puppets. The big question…. Was the war worth fighting?

• • •

On the morning of June 25, 1950, the North Korean Army, known as the Democratic People's Republic of Korea (DPRK), launched an assault across the 38th Parallel with a massive artillery barrage, causing the beginning of the Korean War. The Republic of Korea (ROK) troops were taken by surprise and extremely outnumbered, but retaliated immediately. No match for the north troops, on June 27, Pres. Truman authorized US air and naval operations to support the ROK troops. The first US ground combat troops arrived at Pusan on July 1, 1950, under General Douglas MacArthur's command.

The draft was on at the time and immediately men were being drafted, plus a lot of men joined because they were concerned that America had to do something to stop the Communist aggression.

• • •

From 1911 to 1945, Korea was one country under Japanese control. During World War II, Korea was liberated from the Japanese. After WWII, the United States and Allies agreed with Russia to split the nation in two parts, forming North and South Korea. North Korea would stay under a communist rule of government, while South Korea would be a democracy. It was determined at that time the 38th Parallel would be the line separating the two countries.

By splitting this country, over 10 million people were separated from their families and friends. It caused those of the North to hate those of the South and vice versa. And, it eventually caused the beginning of the not-so-forgotten Korean War.

Korea, including both North and South, is a very mountainous country smaller in area than the state of Wyoming. It has a total area of 85,246 square miles—North Korea 47,071 and South Korea 38,175 square miles. It is located with China (Manchuria) to the north (the Yalu River being the northern border), the Korean Strait to the south, bordering the Yellow Sea on the west coast, and the Sea of Japan on the east coast with 5,400 miles of coastline. Prior to the war, Korea was a country that very few Americans would have known existed, plus even if they had heard of it, they probably wouldn't have known where it was.

• • •

June 25, 1950 was the start of the Korean War, a war that claimed the lives of over 4 million human beings, half civilians, on both sides. It was a war that 1.6 million American troops took part in. It was a war that took the lives of 36,576 American troops; 33,741 by combat, and 2,835 non-combat. It was a war that lasted approximately 3 years and ended only by an armistice agreeable to both sides.

One military historian and Korean War veteran, the late Harry Summer stated, "Although not fully appreciated, the Korean War was one of the most significant wars of the twentieth century. It marked acknowledgement by the Kremlin that communism could no longer be spread by direct force of arms, as it had been spread across eastern Europe in the closing days of World War II."

From June 1950, the US Army had expanded their troops in Korea from 590,000 to over 1,530,000; and the Marine Corp had expanded their forces from 74,279 to 192,620. At first, the American troops didn't have enough troops in Korea to defend against the North and, because of this, were pushed back. Some blame this on the cut back of military troops after WWII, but the draft was on and troops were being trained fast and hard, causing many to still be somewhat green.

It's not hard to see why the United States and their allies were pushed back so fast when Chinese Premier Mao Tse-tung's Chinese troops intervened in the Korean War in support of the North. The US and the UN troops were simply outnumbered.

Though most attention has focused on the Korean War's first year, bloody fighting persisted throughout the entire war. In fact, some 46% of American casualties were sustained between mid-1951 and July of 1953.

In June 1951, the Soviet Union delegate Jacob Malik proposed a cease-fire discussion, and on June 30, 1951, General Ridgeway went on air that the United Nations would be willing to discuss an armistice.

July 10, 1951, armistice talks began. From that time, the war was up and down for the next two years, but still just as deadly. Cease-fires had been declared off and on until July 27, 1953, the day the armistice agreement was finally signed. The "Forgotten War" was finally and officially over. Or, was it?

For decades, the Korean War was regarded as a military defeat at worst and a stalemate at best. But, we who served our time there knew better.

As one former Marine put it, "When I came home from Korea, your family welcomed you and that was it. I never talked about the war. People weren't interested, and they wouldn't have known where it was even if you told them."

Reader's Digest once called Americans who served in Korea "veterans of a forgotten victory."

For the 1.6 million Americans who served in Korea (1950-1953), US society has been less than generous in terms of recognition. It has taken a long time to rectify this injustice and give credit where credit's due.

•   •   •

Did you know that the Korean War was the first armed struggle between Democracy and Communism?

And...

Did you know during the Korean War, the American Armed Forces saved the lives of thousands upon thousands of Korean children?

• • •

A Quote

> *"A veteran, whether active duty, National Guard, or reserve is someone who, at one point in his or her life, wrote a blank check made payable to the United States of America for an amount of up to and including his or her life. That is honor, and there are way too many people in this country who no longer understand it."* — Author Unknown

Cpl. Dennis J. Ottley   *Cpl. Kent K. Ottley*

Photos taken September 1950

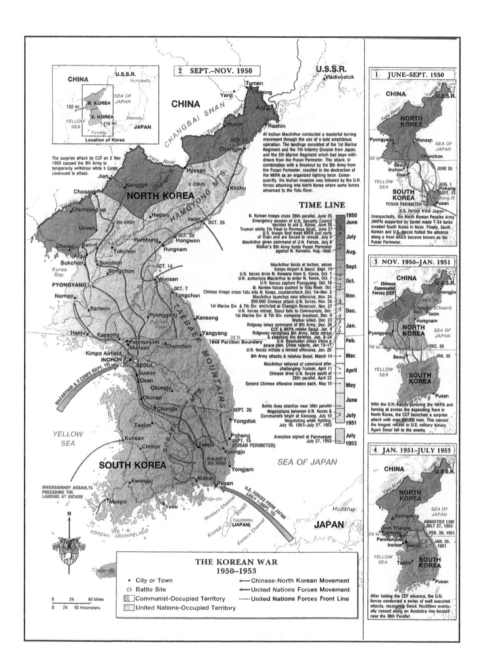

--- REMEMBERING ---

(Korea: 1950-1953)

IT'S THE SOLDIER

It's the Soldier, not the reporter, who has given us the freedom of the press.

It's the Soldier, not the poet, who has given us the freedom of speech.

It's the Soldier, not the politicians, that ensures our right to Life, Liberty And the Pursuit of Happiness.

It's the Soldier who salutes the flag, who serves beneath the flag, And whose coffin is draped by the flag.

IF IT WEREN'T FOR THE MILITARY, THERE'D BE NO UNITED STATES OF AMERICA...

****

CHAPTER 1

EVANSTON TO CAMP CAMPBELL

It was the month of June 1950, when the 141st Tank Battalion of the Wyoming National Guard was on summer guard camp for two weeks at Camp Carson, CO (now known as Fort Carson). Carson was located just south of Colorado Springs, CO. It was a hot and dry summer and grass fires were igniting all over the place, on camp and off camp. We were interrupted from our usual training to assist in fighting the fires. Therefore, after a week or so training with our tanks, we ended up the last few days helping to fight fires.

While at summer camp, the battalion was attached to the 5th Army, which was based at Carson. We remained with the 5th until the 141st tankers were activated in September.

I had joined the guard in November of 1949, mainly because most of my friends had joined and, now, I was at guard camp, training to be a tanker and apparently a firefighter. On about June 22, we completed our summer camp and headed for home.

We were back in Evanston, WY, just a few days before the announcement that North Korea had invaded South Korea. Plus, the announcement that the United States of America would be going to war in support of South Korea. Someone made the statement, "If we had been in Carson a few days longer, or if the North had invaded the South a little sooner, we probably wouldn't have left Carson; we might have been activated right then and there."

At this time, we had no way of knowing how this was going to affect the 141st Tank Battalion, but we knew one way or the other we would be going in the service. If not as a unit, we would probably be drafted separately unless we chose to just join. At this time, the draft was active and going strong.

2

A few weeks later, we got the news that the battalion would be activated and called to duty on September 11, 1950, at which time our unit would be leaving soon for active duty and would be stationed at Camp Campbell, KY. Camp Campbell (now known as Fort Campbell) is located in southwestern Kentucky and northwestern Tennessee on the border between Clarksville, TN, and Hopkinsville (we called it "Hoptown"), KY.

My wife, Sandy, and I had planned to be married on July 26, but after hearing that the guard had gotten orders for active duty, we discussed holding back our plans to be married until I got discharged; but after a lot of thought and discussion, it was decided that we would keep our plans and go ahead and get married. It was strictly Sandy's and my decision. So, we got married as planned on July 26, 1950.

On the day before we left for Campbell, Sandy and I were driving toward town when I, being silly and singing "Mona Lisa" with Sandy sitting next to me, we came to an intersection. Not paying attention to what I was doing, I ran into another car totaling our car completely. It was a bad accident, but fortunately no one was badly hurt and no one was cited or charged for the accident. We had just put brand new tires on the car. I felt really bad about totaling the car because I was going to give it to my folks, who didn't have a car at the time.

Up to that time, we were enjoying ourselves and having fun, knowing that I would be leaving for the army the next morning. But, the accident pretty much ruined the day for us. We called the wrecker and had our car hauled up to Sandy's parents' backyard.

September 23, 1950, Company A of the 141st Tank Battalion was leaving Evanston, a town at that time having a population of about 3,500, for Camp Campbell, KY. We were a bunch of naïve Wyoming kids leaving for the army and possibly Korea.

An advance detail was selected to leave Evanston a few days earlier for Camp Campbell. They left in a convoy with all the vehicles and equipment, plus they picked up additional troops and equipment of other companies from other towns on their route. They headed east on US Highway 30 to Kentucky, a day or two ahead of the rest of us.

The rest of us reported for duty early the morning of September 23 at the National Guard Armory on 6th Street. After all preparations were made and the troops were ready for the trip, we all got information and First Sergeant Wayne Nelson marched us down to the Union Pacific train depot to board the train, calling cadence all the way. Many of the folks in town followed us. It was quite an event.

When we got to the depot, there was a large crowd of local people waiting to see us off. I believe that almost everyone in the county was there. We had a

3

CO.A, 141st TANK BATTALION   SEPTEMBER 11,1950   WYOMING NATIONAL GUARD (EVANSTON)

FRONT ROW, KNEELING
LEFT TO RIGHT: HARLAN ORRELL, FRANCIS T. TAYLOR, LYLE BARNES, EARL BYRNE, ROBERT STADLER,
             WAYNE NELSON, LEONARD MAHLON, CHARLES ALEXANDER, COVEY PAPWORTH.

SECOND ROW, KNEELING
LEFT TO RIGHT: RANOLD PHILLIPS, HARVEY JOHNSTON, FRANK ISHERWOOD JR., TOM RIVERS,
             TERRY CLARK, ROLAND MORANVILLE, JIM BATEMAN, MEL WHITTEAR, PAUL VOSAKIS,
             TOM PASSEY, KENT OTTLEY,

THIRD ROW, KNEELING
LEFT TO RIGHT: TED TAYLOR, WAYNE SLAGOWSKI, BOYD HENDERSON, DUANE DRINKLE, ROY ANDERSON,
             PHIL CARLISLE, CARL WILLIAMS, DENNIS OTTLEY, ALBERT HUGHES,
             MARVIN TREADWAY, JACK MATHSON,

BACK ROW, STANDING
LEFT TO RIGHT: DAVID PASSEY, ELLIS CALDWELL, WAYNE KESSLER, ROBERT STODDARD,
             HARVEY HUTCHINSON, VINCENT CALDWELL, ROBERT MATHSON, WILLIAM KIMBALL,
             MIKE LANE, DEAN CHENEY, LEONARD SIMS, KEITH BROOKS, GEORGE MORRIS,
             RAYMOND TANNER, CLIFF DURRANT,

NOT IN PICTURE: ROBERT KIMBALL,   RALPH LEE.

FIVE EVANSTON BROTHER SETS, ONE FATHER-SON COMBINATION SERVING WITH ARMED FORCES

FORT CAMPBELL, Ky., Nov. 30—Five sets of brothers and one father-son combination are found in "A" company, 141st Tank battalion, now receiving training at Fort Campbell, Ky. Shown in front of one of their medium tanks, they are: (l. to r.) front row: Pfc. Robert and Pfc. William Kimball; Cpl. Dennis and Cpl. Kent Ottley; center row: Cpl. Jack and Cpl. Robert Mathson; Cpl Vincent and Pfc. Ellis Caldwell; back row: SFC Francis Taylor, Sr., and Cpl. Francis Taylor, Jr.; Cpl. Thomas and Pfs. David Passey.

few members from the Bridger Valley area in the guard, and Bridger Valley was also part of Uinta County. As small a population as was available at that time, there was no surprise that everyone would know one another, and most would probably be there.

There were hours of mingling and visiting (hugging and kissing), and believe me there were some ladies that I would just as soon have shaken their hand rather than hug and kiss them. But, it was great to know that all these people were good enough to see us off, and apparently sad to see us going, possibly to war. After all, it hadn't been very long since WWII had ended and the folks still had that on their minds.

The train was now in and we were all ordered to pick up our gear and start boarding. At this moment, Company A of the 141st Tank Battalion was activated and heading east to pick up more troops along the way.

We had members from Star Valley (Afton), Green River, Rock Springs, Rawlins, and Laramie. These communities made up the 141st Tank Battalion of the Wyoming National Guard. The companies were Evanston, Company A; Green River and Rock Springs, Company B; Rawlins, Company C; Star Valley (Afton), Company D; and Laramie was Headquarters Company.

The train was heading east through Wyoming and would be stopping at the other cities to pick up the rest of the battalion. The 141st Tank Battalion was now heading for Camp Campbell, KY, with over 300 troops from Wyoming.

In the Evanston, WY (Company A) group, there were five sets of brothers and one father-son combination; Kent and Dennis Ottley, Robert (Bob) and Jack Mathson, Vincent and Ellis Caldwell, Tom and Dave Passey, and Robert (Bob) and William (Bill) Kimball, plus father and son, Francis (Pappy) and Ted Taylor. In a few weeks, Ellis Caldwell was discharged because of his age (17) and Tom Passey got discharged because of his health.

My brother Kent and I were both promoted to the rank of corporal soon after the battalion was informed of being activated. At that time, corporal was equivalent to the old buck sergeant of WWII, which was no longer a rank. The army discontinued it shortly after the war. Being that both of us were married, this promotion really helped us in our base pay and allotment.

Arriving at Camp Campbell, they marched us to the supply store to pick up our bedding rolls and then we went to a two-story building called the barracks. On each floor there were two rolls of single beds or cots, whatever you wanted to call them. Each bed had a foot locker placed on the floor at the foot of the bed, a place to store our belongings and a rail at the head of the bed on which to hang our uniforms. On the second floor there was one room where the first sergeant, who was in charge, had his quarters and stayed.

The first thing we were taught is how to make our beds or cots, whatever. Everyone was to make them the same, neat and tight. They said they wanted the bed made so tight that you could bounce a quarter off it, and that was how the army wanted it. After making the bed, we found out they were right; the quarter did bounce.

Then they illustrated to us how your foot locker had to be kept and in what order our uniforms had to be hung. Everything was to be kept clean, neat, and uniform, plus we had to keep our boots shined. Most of the time we would give them what we called a "spit shine" where you could damn near see your face in them.

So, we got the opportunity to make up our first army cot and learned how to put our belongings away, and then we went to mess for our first army meal before bedding down. Most everyone was pretty tired after the trip, so they all turned in early. They knew that the first reveille would be coming real early, about 0400 hours (4:00 A.M.). For some reason, waking up and hearing the bugler calling for reveille sounded good. Then the first sergeant came in the barracks calling out, "It's now 4 o'clock, so drop your c——s, and grab your socks," waking everyone, telling us to get up, get dressed, and to fall out in formation in ten minutes just outside the barracks. At that time, we all knew for sure that we were now in the army. After a couple of hours marching and doing some calisthenics, we then went to the mess hall for breakfast.

At first, there was some concern about the 141st being all Wyoming boys and how they would accept the fact that some of their close friends and maybe relatives would be their superiors in army life. For instance, in Company A, Evanston, they all knew one another in civilian life and most went to school together, and might have been good buddies and run around together.

Therefore, some of the officers and non-coms were a little worried about just how the troops would accept the fact that their best friend might have a higher rank and have the authority to give the others orders. But, surprisingly, there were no problems as far as I could tell, at least I had never heard of any. Everyone appeared to get along fine and accept the fact that we were in the army now. Most everyone showed a lot of respect to the ranks and appreciated the other guy's position.

Captain Lyle Barnes was Commanding Officer (CO) of A Company at this time, while Master Sergeant Wayne Nelson was our first sergeant, SFC Charles Alexander was our drill sergeant, MSgt. Francis Taylor (Pappy) was sergeant over the motor pool, and his son SFC Ted Taylor was our mess sergeant. There were also others with higher rank. All these officers and non-coms were from Evanston, so you can see why there would be concern, buddies giving orders to buddies, and in some cases, brothers giving orders to brothers, etc.

7

The 141st Tank Battalion Insignia and Arm Patch...

Motto: Vivions ui Velocique (We live by Force and Speed)

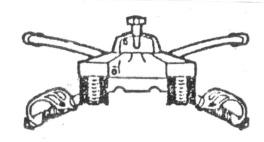

A SHORT HISTORY OF THE 141ST TANK BATTALION
Taken from
Tank Battalions of the U.S. Army
By
James A. SawickiWyvern Publications, 1983

Constituted on the 3rd of December 1941 in the Regular Army as the 641st Tank Battalion. Activated on the 18th of December 1941 at Fort Lewis, Washington, with personnel from the 146th, 148th and 218 Field Artillery Regiments of the 41st Division. Converted, reorganized and re-designated on the 24th of June 1944 as the 98th Chemical Battalion, Motorized. Reorganized and re-designated on the 20th of March 1945 as the 98th Chemical Mortar Battalion. Inactivated on the 26th of December 1945 at Camp Anza, Arlington, California.

Re-designated 141st Tank Battalion and allotted to the Wyoming National Guard on the 29th of July 1946. Organized and Federally recognized 13 February 1947 as the 141st Medium Tank Battalion (120 mm gun). Released from active Federal service and reverted to State control on the 17th of January 1955; concurrently consolidated with the 351st Armored Field Artillery Battalion.

CAMPAIGN STREAMERS
World War II
1. Bismark Archipelago
2. New Guinea
3. Luzon (with arrowhead)
Decorations
Philippine Presidential Unit Citation...

I remember during our first reveille one of the first instructions First Sgt. Wayne Nelson gave us was how to shave. I thought it was kind of ridiculous, but I guess he had his orders. Before we went on the drill, he told us that we had to be clean shaven at all times. That was okay, but when he told us how to shave, going through every little detail, I thought that was a little too much. It was as if nobody had ever shaved before. I thought *just how dumb do they think we were?*

After First Sgt. Nelson got through giving us instructions, SFC Alexander, our drill sergeant, took over and told how we were to stand in formation, whether at ease or at attention. "Stomach in," he'd say, "to where your navel is hitting your spine." He continued, "With chest out and eyes ahead." After a few drills, we all got the message.

We got all the orders—"forward march", "at ease", "double time", "left face", "right face", "about face"—we got them all. I personally kind of enjoyed it, especially when we got to calling cadence. "Stay to the right and you'll never go wrong…", "I don't know, but I've been told…", and many more. Marching, "Hup one, hup two," and so on. "Sound off, 1-2-3-4…", and all that stuff.

So now, we were no longer in the Wyoming National Guard, we were in the army stationed at Camp Campbell, KY, the home of the 11th Airborne Division (the Angels), a well-known airborne division that gained their reputation while fighting in the Pacific and occupying Japan during and after WWII. In 1949, the division moved to Camp Campbell.

I'm not sure what affiliation we had with the 11th Airborne, but if I remember right, we were now under full orders from the 2nd Army. Camp Campbell was also the home of the 2nd Army. We would be doing some of our training with both outfits, and participate in some of the training maneuvers that both were involved in.

It wasn't too long after we got to Campbell when they combined Company D (Star Valley bunch) with Company A and did away with the D Company entirely. That left Companies A, B, C, and Headquarters. Later on, they started bringing in new officers and additional recruits to build up to full strength of what a battalion should be. When we first got to Campbell, we were way short of having enough troops. Most of the new recruits we got in were from the southern states.

At the time we left home, there was no television reception in Evanston, and probably none in most of the towns in Wyoming, especially the smaller communities. So, a lot of the Wyoming kids in the battalion had probably never seen television; I hadn't. I had heard of it, but had never seen it until I got to Campbell. The camp had a television set up in the day room and when we got to spend some time there, it was quite a treat to be able watch TV. Of course, at that time, television was just black and white and sometimes a bit snowy, but we enjoyed it.

The next few weeks, we went mainly into the basic training, some drills and calisthenics, plus policing up the areas. Having the rank of corporal, I never had to pull KP in the mess hall, but I got called quite often for guard duty.

I remember one time when we were doing drills, there must have been about twenty or so troops in the ranks. SFC Charles Alexander was our drill sergeant, and I was in the first roll when he was calling cadence. He yelled out to me and said, "Ottley, get in step." I looked down at my feet hearing the cadence, looked to my right, and I replied back to him and said, "I am in step." So, he looked around and thought for a second and then called us to a halt and about face and said, "I don't know how it happened, but Ottley's right; it's the rest of us that are out of step. So, let's try it again." After the drill, he said that that had to be a first. We laughed.

Camp Campbell had a stockade on base where delinquent soldiers would be put for disciplinary reasons: AWOL, desertion, or something they might have done breaking regulations. I got called to report to the stockade twice for guard duty. Both times, it was an experience that I would never forget.

The first time I was called to take a group of prisoners on a work detail to paint benches at the ballpark. I was assigned to this detail with another soldier from another unit because there were so many prisoners. How many guards you have depends on how many prisoners there are. The prisoners were considered what they called "trustees," so they got to do duty outside the stockade.

While you are on duty guarding prisoners on a work detail outside of the stockade, you are armed with a .45-caliber automatic pistol and an M1 carbine, both with live ammo. Being new to guard duty at the stockade, we weren't sure what to do in case a prisoner tried to escape while they were under our jurisdiction.

So, we asked, and they told us that if any prisoner attempted to escape, we should do whatever it took to stop them, even if it meant shooting them. They said that is why we were armed. They told us that if any of the prisoners escaped, we would be put in the stockade in their place until they were caught. I hoped they were just kidding; they were.

Well, we were thankful that they all ended up being trustworthy, because if any of them had tempted to escape, I'm not so sure what I would have done to try and stop them. I had never shot at anyone before, and I wasn't sure they were so bad that they should be shot.

The second time I was called for guard duty at the stockade, I had to check my weapons in because I was called to stand guard just inside the main gate. When on guard duty inside the compound, you aren't allowed to be armed.

While I was there guarding the main gate, I witnessed something that I thought was strange and uncalled for.

There was a prisoner sitting on the steps of one of the barracks when one of the regular guards, a sergeant who was in charge, walked over to him and started getting on him for something he was supposed to have done. The prisoner tried to tell him that he hadn't done anything wrong. The guard got real angry and started hollering and cussing at the prisoner, using strong language. The hollering got my attention, so I took notice of what was going on. There was nothing that I could do about it, so I just watched.

The prisoner asked the guard what he had done, but the guard wouldn't even listen to him. He just handcuffed the prisoner and brought him toward the main gate. The guard then had the prisoner stop at one of the guy-wires used to brace the light poles in the yard. The guy-wire supporting the pole was a heavy cable with a turn buckle that was used to tighten or loosen the cable. The turn buckle was a good size, but it wasn't big enough for what the guard wanted the prisoner to do. At that time, I witnessed something that I thought was uncalled for and out of order.

The guard ordered the prisoner, still handcuffed, to get on his knees facing the turn buckle of the cable, and told him to put his head through the center of it. Well, there was no way in hell he could have done that; the buckle only had about an inch and a half opening. So, not being able to do what he was told to do, the sergeant started banging the buckle against the head of the prisoner. He did this for several minutes, telling the prisoner to put his head through the buckle, screaming at him. I didn't see any blood, so I'm not sure just how hard he was hitting him with the buckle, but I know it couldn't have felt very good. I was beginning to feel sorry for the prisoner, but there was nothing I could do. I had no jurisdiction inside the stockade.

The sergeant finally stopped, and I was told that he took the prisoner to the area where they keep the hardcore prisoners and threw him in solitary confinement. I felt really bad for the prisoner at that time, but later on, we found out that the stockade had been under investigation for mistreatment of prisoners and other violations. Apparently, the prisoner that I witnessed being mistreated was an undercover agent placed in the stockade as a plant to find out what was going on. When I heard that, I really had to admire him for taking all that abuse.

After the investigation was over, they closed the stockade and took all the prisoners to another facility until they could get the situation under control. I never heard what happened to the personnel involved, but after the investigation was over, they opened the stockade up again. I don't recall who it was turned over to for operation, but it was probably either the 2nd Army or the 11th Airborne.

I'm not sure who the operation of the stockade was under prior to the investigation, but fortunately I never got assigned to guard duty there again. I was glad about that. I wasn't too fond about having to guard GIs, delinquent or not; it just didn't feel right. Most of them appeared to be alright guys and pretty trustworthy.

The post also had what they called "the Bird Cage" on base. It was a large area with a lot of acreage, completely fenced in with a high chain-link fence and barbed wire strung at the top, very secure. They told us that it was a very secretive and classified experimental area, never said exactly what they did there, but they did say to try to stay away from the area. I never did find out what it was all about, which was alright with me; I really didn't care. We never did hang around that area much, unless we were on drill or something. Whatever it was, it was something that was pretty hush-hush.

Cpl. Dennis Ottley
ready for guard duty at the
Stockade in Campbell…

Cpl. Dennis Ottley and
Cpl. Jack Mathson resting
after policing up the area
at Campbell…

Cpl. Robert "Bob" Mathson in class "A" uniform ready for leave.

Cpl. Duane Drinkle in class "A" ready for leave.

Left to right: PFC George Morris, Cpl. Mike Lane, SSgt Harvey Johnston, Cpl. William "Bill" Kimball, Cpl. Jack Mathson, SSgt Ralph Lee, Cpl. Keith Brooks and Cpl. Dennis Ottley, all on leave in Hoptown (Hopkinsville).

Cpl. Dennis Ottley

Cpl. Jack Mathson

CHAPTER 2

SANDY'S VISIT TO CAMPBELL

My brother's wife, Melba, and my wife, Sandy, decided to come out to Campbell to visit us for a few weeks in October. When they arrived, it was quite a surprise to me, because I had no idea Sandy was coming. Plus, I had no idea how she could afford the trip. After asking her how she did it, she told me that she sold the tires on our wrecked car, and that was where she got the money to make the trip. Anyway, I was damn glad to see her.

Sandy and I had no money to speak of and neither one of our folks had any money, so it really surprised me that she was there. Kent was in a little different situation than I was. His in-laws were in pretty good shape where they could afford to help Melba make the trip. Regardless, we both were glad to see them.

They were able to stay on the base for a few days while we looked for a place to rent. While on base, they got to watch the troops marching, calling cadence, etc. Sandy said she loved watching and hearing them. She had never seen anything like that before. She would have liked to stay on base for the rest of her visit, but it wasn't allowed, so they had to go to Clarksville, TN, to look for an apartment.

After a couple days, we finally found them a place in Clarksville to rent for a while. Both of the girls were pregnant at the time, so Kent and I both were expecting our first child. I believe Melba was a month or so further along than Sandy was.

Melba, being about three years older than Sandy, and having relatives in Arkansas, knew more about the South than Sandy did. Sandy was only 17 at the time and still pretty naïve about life. She had spent all her life in Evanston, not having much of a chance to learn about the rest of the world. While in

Clarksville, she had an incident happen that was quite a learning lesson for her, and when hearing about it, I thought it was quite humorous.

Sandy and Melba got on the bus in Clarksville to go somewhere. They found a seat on the bus, but when an older and feeble black lady (called Negroes at the time) with her arms full of groceries, got on the bus and there were no seats left. Sandy made the big mistake of getting up and offering her seat to the woman. I guess everyone on the bus came unglued and got really upset at Sandy, including the black lady she was trying to help. The bus driver was so mad he kicked both Melba and Sandy off the bus and called the police. At that time, black folks had to sit in the back of the bus, but at this particular time, there were no seats left and the lady had to stand.

I guess when the police came they wondered what two young girls would be doing and what happened. They asked for identification, but Sandy didn't drive at that time, so she didn't have a driver's license or any other kind of ID. Melba had her driver's license and explained that they were from Wyoming where there was no prejudice like in the South. She told them that Sandy had never been around that sort of thing. They also explained that they were there visiting their husbands stationed at Camp Campbell. After the police left, I guess they caught another bus and finished what they were doing. Before they got on the other bus, Melba told Sandy that she should sit down and keep her mouth shut.

That was a real experience for my wife, for she had never been any place where people were so biased against a minority like they were in the South. We only had one black person in Evanston at the time and everybody in town treated him just like everyone else. So, it wasn't too hard to understand Sandy's reason for doing what she did, but she never did it again, not while she was there, at least.

While they were there, Kent and I got some leave time, so we got to spend some time off base with our wives. There were other wives there also. PFC Frank Isherwood and his wife, Jesse, Cpl. Ralph Lee and his wife, Marion, and Cpl. Keith Brooks and his wife, Isabel, were all there. We all got to spend quite a bit of time with them, taking them around, looking at the sights, and eating at different restaurants...just enjoying ourselves. However, after a couple of weeks, Sandy and I couldn't afford to have her stay any longer, so she and Melba caught the train and went home, back to Evanston, WY.

After a while Kent's wife, Melba, came back and got an apartment where Kent could live off base some of the time. Of course, he had to report for duty a lot so most of the time he had to stay on base. It all depended on what his duties were. In fact, Melba had her first baby, Nikki, on camp at the base hospital. Kent had also gotten a promotion to staff sergeant while she was there.

That helped their financial situation out a little with him getting an additional raise in his base pay.

There was no way that Sandy and I could afford her coming to live near the base, so she stayed home and had our first baby, Randy, at the county hospital in Evanston in June 1951. She could have gone to Salt Lake City, UT, to have the baby at Fort Douglas and let the army pay for it, but it would have been a real inconvenience for her to do that. We had no car. Sandy didn't drive, at that time, so we would have had to depend on someone else and we didn't want to do that.

When you are in Kentucky, you would think there would be a lot of Kentucky bluegrass; in the Camp Campbell area, there didn't seem to be much of the bluegrass. Most of the grass we found to be what we called onion grass. This was in the lawns and yards at the camp. It smelled like onions and it had the onion taste. Matter of fact, the milk cows in the area must have fed off the onion grass, because the milk we drank and used on our cereal had the same taste. It wasn't just the milk; it was other foods that also had the same taste. Because of it, some of the foods weren't very good, but it was all we had.

After being there a while, we noticed that there was quite a difference from the West, not only in the climate, but also in the lifestyle. The elevation at the camp was only about 400 feet, where in Evanston it was right at 6,700 feet, a big difference. Evanston is right in the middle of the Rocky Mountains. The winters were quite a lot longer at home and we always had more snow than the South, but the climate was very dry. The South had a very damp and humid climate, which made it feel a lot colder. Our summers were shorter and cooler. In the summer, it seldom got above 85 degrees. The summers in the South get pretty hot, 100 degrees or more sometimes; plus, it also is damp and humid.

Also, the lifestyle was a little different in some ways. I came to find that some foods were different. There were some that I had never heard of, such as grits, but Sandy had; she ate them and loved them. Every once in a while she'd fix them at home.

We found the towns and communities were closer together and more populated with heavier traffic. In Wyoming, the towns are much further apart. Wyoming was noted as the state with the wide open spaces. At the time, I think there were less than 400,000 people in the entire state.

We also found that the South had a lot of chiggers. They live in the grass, so you had to be careful where you sat or laid, because if you got them on you, they would get into your skin and drive you nuts, itching and scratching. They are a real tiny mite and hard to see (we called them "NO SEE 'EMs"). That was our way of describing them. So, you had to be careful where you sat or laid on the grass. There were lots of them right in camp, so we found out real quick where not to lie. In Wyoming, we never had them. I guess it was too cold.

Fireflies were something that we had never seen before, but we thought they were fun to watch at night. They never seemed to bother anyone, they just flew around at night in bunches, all lit up. They were actually pretty neat. We came to find out that there were a lot more insects and spiders in the South than there are at home. I guess it is because of the hot climate.

The area also had a lot more different species of snakes than we had in Wyoming. We were told that there were no rattlesnakes, but there were what they called the water moccasin. Apparently, it was the only poisonous snake in the area. They told us that we should watch out for the moccasin, especially around water and marshy areas.

Wyoming had rattlesnakes in most areas of the state, but there weren't any around Evanston. The only snake that I ever saw around home was the garter snake, some called it the water snake, and they were harmless. It was strange that we didn't have any rattlesnakes in the county, because they had them about 20 miles west of Evanston into Utah and 100 miles east of Evanston in the Rock Springs area.

One of the new recruits that was from the South tried to tell us that the water moccasin would never bite at night, but one of the locals told us that was a lot of bull, that they would bite anytime.

By now, Sandy had gone home to Evanston and would be living with her folks, at least until the baby was born. I wouldn't see her again until Christmas. That is, if I was lucky enough to get a furlough at that time. I sure hoped so.

Corporal Dennis Ottley - 1950

Sandy and Cpl. Dennis Ottley - 1950

CHAPTER 3

IN THE FIELD

We were into November now and a lot of new recruits, mostly draftees, had been coming in and were being assigned to the 141st to help bring the battalion up to full strength. We got a new commanding officer, but that wasn't anything new; it seemed like we had a new CO quite often. Captain Lyle Barnes was no longer CO of Company A. He was now at headquarters.

We also had a lot of new officers coming in to help fulfill the battalion needs. Some of these officers were out of the reserves and some were regular army. Most of the recruits were from the southern states, and they were all a bunch of great guys and fit right in with us Wyoming boys.

Now that we had the battalion at full strength, or close to it, we started big in field training with the tanks and small arms. We went on several bivouacs with the M4 Sherman tanks for training. We practiced shooting the 76 mm tank gun and the attached machine guns. Everyone had to learn the different positions on a tank: driving, gunnery, loading the big gun, firing machine guns, plus operating the radio. The positions in a tank were: tank commander, driver, gunner, loader (of the cannon), and assistant driver, sometimes called the bow gunner, because he had a .30-caliber machine gun mounted in front of him for his use, when needed. My MOS (Military Occupational Specialist) ended up being tank driver, which I enjoyed and was good at, but I also learned to fire the big gun and I got to be pretty good at that, too.

I thought it was very interesting being a tanker and really enjoyed it. I was assigned to the tank dozer as a driver for a short time. The dozer was an M4 Sherman tank with a big snow blade. It also had the 76 mm cannon. Sometimes we would be called out to get a tank out from being stuck or broke down, or we would be called out to do a little excavating or clearing an area, where needed. We even plowed a little snow that winter.

Some would think there's no way you could get a tank stuck, but it does happen occasionally. I have seen several tanks stuck, especially in swampy areas. I got stuck once along with a lot of others while we were on bivouac performing an experimental operation called "Operation Miller." This happened later on in the spring of the next year.

One time, during night maneuvers, Cpl. Paul Vozakis drove his tank into a large hole in the ground that we all thought had been an old cellar for a house one time or other. Vozakis couldn't see the cellar because it was a very dark night, and nobody had told anyone that the hole was there. When they hit the hole, it had to be a hell of a jolt. I heard that it took more than one tank to get him out.

Although the M1 rifle wasn't one of our assigned weapons, we still had to spend some time on the firing range. I got a few Maggie's drawers (what they call it when you miss a target completely; they wave a red flag from the pit that looks like Maggie's drawers), but I still ended up doing pretty well. Now, when it came to the pistol, I had a hell of a time hitting anything with the .45-caliber automatic, which was the pistol all GIs carried as a sidearm. It was the only small arms weapon in the military that had the left-handed spiral in the barrel. They said it was built that way because it had such a kick to it. They also said that was why a lot of GIs had such a hard time with it. I told my instructor that I would be better off just throwing the damn thing at the enemy rather than trying to shoot him. The instructor just laughed and said, "You'll learn," and after a few times on the range, I did.

We practiced a lot with the .30-caliber machine gun and some with the .50-caliber. The .30-caliber was mounted in the turret and in front of the assistant driver's (bog-gunner) seat, and the .50-caliber was mounted on top of the turret. The .50 was used a lot in case of an air attack.

The only small arms weapons that were assigned to a tank were one .30-caliber M2 carbine and one .45-caliber machine gun, which we called a grease gun, because it looked similar to those hand grease guns we used to lubricate our cars with at home. We had to go through the firing range and learn to fire these weapons also. I did well with both weapons.

The only weapon that was assigned personally to a tanker was the .45-caliber automatic pistol and, during combat, you had to keep that on you at all times, except when you were sleeping, and then you better keep it close. The only other weapon that we had on our person was the trench knife, which some called the bayonet.

In the army, you never called a pistol or rifle a gun. If you did and a non-com heard you, they would say to you, "This is your rifle (or pistol)," holding

M-4 Sherman TankDozer with the 76 mm. cannon
Left to right: PFC James Bateman Cpl. Dennis Ottley and PFC Marvin Treadway

Tank Dozer

SSgt. Harvey Johnston, Cpl. Ralph Lee and Cpl. Duane Drinkle With full pack

Cpl. Keith Brooks in the field

Cpl. Mike Lane with full pack

it out, "This is your gun," (pointing to your fly). "This is for business," (again holding your weapon), "this is for fun," (again, pointing to your fly). And, they never let you forget it, and nobody ever did.

We also had to learn how to shoot the bazookas. They weren't part of the tank weapons, but I guess the army wanted every GI to learn about all weapons, just in case the situation changed. Firing the bazooka was pretty interesting...how it was done. They were much different than the rest of the small arms weapons.

It took two GIs, one to hold and aim the weapon and one to load it. Once the loader had shoved the shell in the bazooka, he would pat the other on the head to let him know that it was loaded, ready to fire, and he was in the clear, because it had a terrific back blast. In fact, the bazooka was one of the weapons that tankers had to look out for. Certain types could wipe out a tank.

We practiced throwing the hand grenade. Unlike the firing ranges where the ammo was real, the grenades were only practice types that would explode and just smoke. We got behind a panel about shoulder high, they pointed out a target, then they told us to throw the grenade like a football and try to hit that target. They also instructed us to make sure we got down low after we threw it. This was to teach you to fall flat when you threw a grenade in combat, because when it explodes, it sprays upward in a cone-shape pattern.

One of the most hazardous training programs we went through was the infiltration course. They shot .30-caliber machine guns with live ammo about 3 feet above the ground and you had better keep your ass down. We had to crawl on our bellies through the course and we did it twice. The first time, we did it in about 3 inches of mud, and the second time was in about 3 inches of snow. The first time we were so muddy after we got through the course, when we got back to the barracks, we had to take off our fatigues before entering. The second time, we were just wet and damn cold.

Why they claimed the infiltration course as being one of the most dangerous programs in training and most hazardous is because they used live ammo and sometimes accidents happen. For instance, a few weeks after our outfit went through the program, there was a pretty bad and fatal accident that happened on the same course.

Apparently, one of the tripods to one of the machine guns had collapsed, killing a couple GIs, and wounding a few. From what we heard, it was a bunch from the 11th Airborne that was involved. We also heard that there was a big investigation over it, but we never heard any more; nonetheless, it did actually happen.

However, the training schedule that I felt was one of the worst was going through the gas chamber; some called it the gas shack. It was a small building with one room. When you went through it you were to enter the front door with your gas mask on and then you would approach a table where someone was sitting with a gas mask on and a paper pad and a pen lying in front of him on the table. As soon as you approached him, you were to remove your mask and then state your name, rank, and serial number. That wouldn't be a good time to forget your serial number. If you did, God help you, because as soon as you stated your name, rank, and number, you were ready to hit that back door and get the hell out of there for some fresh air. The gas wasn't only burning your eyes; it was also affecting your breathing. It was bad. During this time, we were also doing a lot of training on the tanks. We were going out on a lot of tank maneuvers and mock assaults, supporting various infantry units from the 2nd Army and the 11th Airborne, sometimes camping and staying overnight. During these maneuvers, we were using the M4 A3 E8 "Sherman" medium tank with the 76 mm gun.

We went through this type of training all through the winter and into the spring. It was a cold and wet winter with a heavier snow fall than usual. Some of the locals said (jokingly) that the reason for more snow than usual that winter was because of us (the Wyoming bunch), claiming we brought it there from Wyoming. That area apparently didn't normally get that much snow fall during their winters. The locals, along with the troops, had a lot of fun kidding around about that.

· · ·

When we entered the military service, we had to take an oath. That oath is as follows:

> I, (name), do solemnly swear (or affirm) that I will support and defend the Constitution of the United States, against all enemies, foreign and domestic; that I will bear true faith and allegiance to the same; and that I will obey the orders of the President of the United States and the orders of the officers appointed over me, according to regulations and the Uniform Code of Military Justice. So help me God.

· · ·

One day we were scheduled to go out in the field for more training and maneuvering with the tanks, but apparently the tracks on the tanks had torn up some of the roads and caused a lot of damage to the turf in some areas the previous time out, so they canceled the training for that day. I guess the post commander got a little upset and ordered us to take our tanks to the motor pool where they covered the steel tracks with rubber liners so the tracks wouldn't tear up the roads so much. I suppose it did the trick, but I don't think it would have been a very good idea if we had been in real combat.

So, the next time we went out with the Sherman tanks for training, we used the rubber track liners so it wouldn't cause so much damage. The rubber liners proved to work pretty well, but we sure didn't have the traction that we were used to, especially off the road.

The M4 A3 E8 Sherman medium tank came out of production in early 1944 and was used during the last half of WWII. Although it could not compete on a one-on-one basis with the German tanks (Panthers and Tigers), it was the best that America had at that time. Some called it the "Super Sherman" because of its powerful 76 mm gun with a tremendous muzzle speed and firing range a maximum distance of approximately 15,000 yards. This was the best America had until the M46 models came out. The M4 and M46 were both used in Korea.

The M46 Patton had the 90 mm gun and weighed 46 ton while the M4 had the 76 mm gun and was only 34.8 ton. Also, the M46 had a speed of 30 mph, but only a range of 80 miles. The M4 had a speed of only 26 mph with a range of 100 miles. Both tanks had a 5-man crew with the same positions. The Sherman held 75 rounds of 76 mm ammo, while the Patton held 70 rounds of 90 mm ammo. Both tanks had two .30-caliber machine guns and one .50-caliber mounted on top. Korea was the first war the M46 was used in.

We spent a good share of that winter out in the field, practicing tank maneuvers and firing the tank guns. We all got to where we could handle the M4 Sherman pretty well, but after hearing about the new M46 Patton tank, we were waiting and getting pretty anxious to see what the Patton would be like.

We were told that the big difference, besides the size and the bigger gun, was that the M46 never had the old tank levers to drive with. It just had what they called a toggle stick that you would just move around to go whichever way you wanted, plus it was able to turn around on a dime, or precisely speaking, in the middle of an intersection, where it took the Sherman almost a whole block to make a 360 degree turnaround. After getting the Patton tanks, we came to find out that they were right. There was an amazing difference in driving the two tanks.

After a while, we were told that we would be receiving the new M46 Patton sometime after the first of the year. We were all very anxious to see what they were like. I was officially a tank driver now and I was really excited about driving one of the new tanks and testing out one of those toggle sticks that we heard about. I was also looking forward to firing the 90 mm gun that was

31

mounted on the Patton. We had heard that it had a much stronger and louder muzzle blast than the 76 mm.

After we completed that portion of our field training and returned to our barracks, a bunch of my buddies and I decided to go to Nashville as soon as we got paid and were able to get a weekend pass. Sandy had already gone back to Wyoming by this time. When we got to Nashville, some of the guys wanted to go to this nice restaurant and have a steak dinner with a baked potato. Up to this time, I had never had a steak dinner and hadn't even known what a baked potato was; let alone what it tasted like. Mike Lane, one of my buddies from Wyoming, suggested I try out an oyster cocktail, which I had never heard of, but being game, I ordered one not knowing whether or not I would like it. I didn't and haven't had one since, but the steak and baked potato were great.

After eating, some of the guys wanted to go and get tattoos, something that a lot of GIs had. Most of the guys I was with refused, but went with the others while they got theirs. I told them that tattoos were too permanent for me and, as far as I was concerned, the only thing in life that should be considered permanent is death. Also, I couldn't see applying something on my body that I wouldn't want to have seen on my car or my house, if I had either. So, most of us passed on that venture, but afterwards, we all went and had a few drinks then went back to camp.

Cpl. Dennis Ottley and others washing their mess gears after chowing down

Cpl. Dennis Ottley, Cpl. Bill Kimball and PFC Frank Isherwood chowing down in the field

Cpl. Jack Mathson and others balting 30 cal. ammo

Cpls. Dennis Ottley and Mike Lane in the field

Cpl. Dennis Ottley on the ammunition truck

"Winter at Camp Campbell"
Troops shoveling snow around barracks

Cpl. Dennis Ottley shoveling snow in front of barracks

Note: the shovels

Cpl. Paul Vozakis, SSgt. Boyd Henderon, Cpl. Jack Mathson and others shoveling snow

M.4 sherman tanks on the road

CHAPTER 4

141ˢᵀ GOES ATHLETIC

Before the 141ˢᵗ Tankers were called to active duty, I had done a lot of boxing through my junior and senior high school years. I had fought in the ring a couple dozen times before going into the army. I loved boxing and had been entering the ring since I was 13 years old. So, when the bulletin came out from headquarters that they were going to have boxing on camp, I immediately signed up.

However, before I signed up, I first had to make an appointment with the post dentist because of having terrible toothaches. After the dentist looked at my teeth and had x-rays taken, they came to find out that three of my upper front teeth were cracked in the roots and that they had to come out.

Apparently, sometime during my boxing, they had been cracked from getting hit so much in the mouth. During that time, we never had the best of equipment and mouthpieces were never available. Sometimes, I would chew gum to help keep my mouth shut while in the ring, but I never used a mouthpiece until I was in the army. I guess that's probably why my upper front teeth were so bad.

After the x-rays were taken, my next visit to the dentist he sat me in the chair and while looking at my teeth, he had a pair of dental pliers in his hand and grabbed one front tooth with them. I thought he was going to just try to loosen the tooth, but when he jerked real hard and pulled that tooth out, I came off of that seat about three feet. He took me by surprise and it hurt like hell. That was the most painful moment I'd ever had in my life up to that time. The other two teeth he deadened before pulling, thank God. But that first tooth, although it was awfully painful when he pulled it, it only hurt for a short time.

I was previously warned that army doctors and dentists were never very easy or sympathetic on a GI when it came to administering pain. I guess they thought we should be man enough to take it. I was told later that the tooth was infected so badly that the dentist didn't think it would be good to use a pain killer, but he did on the next two...thank God!

The dentist then made me a partial plate to replace the teeth he had pulled. I had a hard time getting used to wearing the plate, but without it, I looked like a Jack O'Lantern. All my buddies kind of laughed at me when I didn't have the plate in.

I finally got the chance to sign up for the boxing program. I joined with about six other Wyoming boys, plus a few of the new recruits that came in, but I was the only one that stayed with it. On the first day when we all reported for training, we met the coach/trainer and the rest of the team, only to find that the entire team was all black guys, except those from the 141st. I don't know whether this had any bearing on it, but for some reason or other, some of the Wyoming boys changed their minds and just quit on the spot. Then, a few days later the rest of them quit, including all the new recruits. So, I was the only one from the 141st that remained on the team, leaving me the only white guy. Well, that didn't bother me much because I really wanted to box. After a few practice days, I ended up qualifying for the welterweight division.

The coach/trainer was also black. He was from the Chicago area and had fought professionally before entering the service. He was a pretty good coach and knew his business, but he never paid much attention to me and never did work my corner during my fights as my second, or as my trainer. I always had to get someone from the 141st to work my corner. My brother Kent sometimes helped me and a Lt. Brimhall from Afton, WY, helped me a couple times as my second in the corner. Lt. Brimhall was a former boxer and knew a lot about it.

However, the coach did have me sparring with the others, but never had much to do with me during training. He never talked to me much, never criticized me, or gave me any advice that might have helped me improve myself. I had no idea why he was that way, unless it was because I was white. I know I wasn't the best fighter on the team, but I know I wasn't the worst, either. I had the opportunity to spar with each member of the team in training and had no trouble handling myself against any of them. They were all good sports and easy to get along with. It just seemed like none of them wanted to have much to do with me. I found out real fast how it felt to be the minority, but that was okay, because other than trying to help me, they treated me alright, and I got to like them a lot.

The best thing about participating in sports while in the army is that you never have to pull KP or any guard duty. One reason was because of the training you were required to do every day. It didn't matter what sport you entered, whether it be boxing, wrestling, baseball, or basketball, you were never required to pull any other special duties. In the army it was considered a privilege to participate in sports.

The camp's boxing program included several teams with which we had to box for elimination. After two losses, you would be eliminated. Our team was number five. I'm not sure how many teams there were on base, but if and when you lost your second match, you were eliminated. Each match was for three 3-minute rounds, and if you weren't in shape, that was a long time. Actually, it was a long time even if you were in shape. The winners of the different weight divisions automatically got to go to the tournament in Fort Mead, MD, for the "All Army" championship. I was hoping I could make it, but it didn't work out that way.

My first boxing match was on November 17, 1950, at the Camp Campbell field house against a member of the 511th Airborne Infantry named Atkinson. I won the match by a technical knockout in the 2nd round. Feeling real good about the win, I thought my chances of winning the post championship might be pretty good. I got to admit, though, while that was my first fight on new ground, I was a bit worried and scared of how I might do.

My next fight was on November 24 against another airborne trooper by the name of Martinez (I hope it's spelled right). He had won his first fight by a knockout the same night that I had fought and won. He knocked his opponent out in the 2nd round. He was a little Hispanic guy that appeared to be a strong fighter with a good punch. I fought him in my second match and he ended up knocking me out, also in the 2nd round. That was the first and only time in my boxing career that I had ever been knocked out for the full count. I had him on points the first round, but he caught me with a left hook the second round and put me away for the count. Laying there on the canvas, all I could remember was seeing the light above me keep going round and round and round.

After hearing about Martinez taking the post championship, I didn't feel too bad because he knocked out every one of his opponents to get there. He ended up going to Fort Mead, but I never heard how he did. He was a strong fighter with one hell of a left hook.

My last fight on the post was with a fancy boxer that Martinez had knocked out in his first fight. He was taller and had me on reach. I had a hard time with him because I had to chase him all over the ring. I guess because he got knocked out his first fight, he wasn't going to take a chance on getting knocked out again. He was a pretty good boxer, but with him retreating all the time, I had a hard time boxing him, so consequently, he beat me by a close decision.

Although very disappointed in my first year of army boxing, I was looking forward to trying out again the next season, but I never got to because the next year I was in Korea. I got to thinking about staying in the army another hitch so I could participate in boxing again sometime.

About this time, the 141st was planning on participating in the post basketball program. The team was composed of some former players from the University of Wyoming, but most were former players that were damn good and had played Wyoming high school ball. They were under the coaching of Lt. L. D. Johnson from Laramie, WY. They played different units on the post to get to the post finals. The 141st did very well all through the tournament with no losses and ended up taking the post championship.

Brig. Gen. L. Mathewson, commanding general at Camp Campbell, presented battalion colors to Lt. Col. Louis A. Hansen from Laramie, WY, following a post review on January 6, 1951. After the review, the tankers learned that they had been selected as the best marching unit by the inspecting general and his staff.

Twenty one "Red-eye Dicks" of the 141st Tankers scored as "expert" with the .45-caliber automatic pistol while firing on the range. Cpl. Darald Erickson from Afton, WY, scored the highest with a 309 out of a possible 350. Those making a score of 280 or above were qualified as expert. Included in this group were Cpl. Ralph Lee and PFC Floyd Rivers, both from Evanston, WY. I didn't do very well with the .45 handgun, but I did score high with the rifle.

Quite a few members of the 141st did well on other firing ranges. Several scored well with the M1 rifle, the M2 carbine, and also the big gun, the 76 mm cannon. Some of the tank gunners scored great with the big gun. I was one of those gunners.

Some of tankers participated in quite a few educational programs on post and at Fort Knox for different classes and seminars. I recall Cpl. Ralph Lee from Evanston receiving his diploma as a graduate of the discussion leader's course conducted by the Camp Campbell Information and Education Center, making him qualified to conduct the weekly Troop Information hour for others.

At the graduation ceremony, the post executive officer underlined the importance of I & E work. The 40-hour course teaches discussion techniques and is given to selected men from various companies.

41

Dennis Ottley's boxing photo
used on posters in civilian life

Evanston Men Figure In Fort Campbell Events

1950

FORT CAMPBELL, Ky., Nov. 22—At a graduation ceremony last week Pvt. Robert R. Lee, "A" company, 141st Tank battalion, received his diploma as a graduate of the discussion leaders course conducted by the Ft. Campbell information and education center. He is now qualified to conduct the weekly Troop Information hour in his company.

At the graduation ceremony Monday, November 13, Col. Nadal, post executive officer, underlined the importance of I&E work.

The 40-hour course teaches discussion techniques and is given to picked men from various companies.

Evanston Boxer Wins

Cpl. Dennis J. Ottley, "A" Co., 141st Tank bn., scored a technical knockout over his opponent. Pvt. Atkinson of the 511th Airborne Inf., in the second round of their fight Friday night, Nov. 17 at the Ft. Campbell field house. He fought in the welterweight division.

Cpl. Ottley, whose home is in Evanston, represented Boxing Team No. 5 on the post and will probably fight again on Nov. 24 and Dec. 1.

Qualify as Expert Pistolmen

Twenty-one "Read-eye Dicks" of the 141st Tank bn. scored as "expert" with the cal. .45 automatic pistol in recent arms qualifications firing on the range. Highest score made was 309 out of a possible 350, made by Cpl. Darald N. Erickson, "D" company. Lt. Col. Louis A. Hansen, battalion commander, and Pfc. Clyde Hohnholt, Hq and Sv. Co., were tied for the runner-up position with 304 points each. Those making a score of 280 or above were qualified as expert.

Included in this group are Pvt. Robert R. Lee, 283, and Pvt. Floyd F. Rivers, 293, of Co. A.

CHAPTER 5

FIRST FURLOUGH, CHRISTMAS

The holidays were near and we were all hoping for a furlough. Most of the troops from Wyoming did get the ten-day furlough for the Christmas holidays. Bob and Jack Mathson, Mike Lane, Keith Brooks, and I, plus others caught the bus out of Hoptown (Hopkinsville) to Chicago, where we got on the train for Evanston, WY. The train took us right to the depot in Evanston where our wives, family, and friends were waiting. It felt great to be home after being gone almost four months.

At that time, Sandy was staying with her folks. We stayed there all through my furlough and I enjoyed having spent the time visiting with my in-laws. Her dad and I talked a lot about what my training was like and how I liked the tanks. He had never been in the service, but was very patriotic and seemed very proud that I was serving. He was, like my dad, too young for WWI and too old for WWII.

My mother and Grant, my adopted father, were still living in Evanston, along with my sister Terry and her husband, Johnny, and my two younger brothers Mack and Bob. Kent, my older brother, who was in the service with me, didn't go back to Evanston on his furlough. He and his wife, Melba, were living in Clarksville, TN, at this time. His wife was getting pretty big with their first baby, so they decided to stay there for the holidays.

While I was home, I spent some time visiting with my mother and Grant. Mom was worried about me having to go to Korea. I told her not to worry that, so far, there had been no indication that either Kent or I would be going overseas. However, when I got back to camp the next spring, I did get orders for Korea. Kent stayed in the states. Ever since my best friend Paul Oaks had gotten killed in North Korea in November of 1950, Mom had been worried about me and Kent being sent over to Korea to fight. Paul wasn't only my friend; he was also very close to my entire family, especially Mom, who thought an awful lot of him.

Sandy was about three months along with our first child, but we did go out on the town a few nights and enjoyed ourselves. We went out dancing and drinking at Pete's Rock-N-Rye Club a couple times, plus we took in a few teenage dances that the Eagles Club put on for the kids. After all, Sandy and I were still kids, ourselves, 17 and 18 years old. We didn't have a car, so we didn't go out of town to anywhere special; we just stayed home and visited with our family and friends.

It was fun being home and I was dreading the time when I had to go back. I enjoyed the army, but I would have rather stayed home with my wife, especially while she was pregnant. I knew there was no way that I was going to be able to be home when our baby was born, and this had me concerned. I knew I had to go back, that there was no way of getting out of it. Hell, I probably wouldn't have tried getting out of it even if there had been a way; I felt obligated to stay in, at least for my term.

Well, our furlough was over and we were due back in camp by the morning of January 2, so we all caught the train at Evanston, which would take us back through Chicago where we would catch the bus back to Hoptown (Hopkinsville, KY). When we got to the "Windy City" (Chicago), we found out that we would have about a 4-hour layover before the bus was due to take us south to Hopkinsville.

So, to kill time, we thought we would walk around downtown Chicago and visit places like the theatre that John Dillinger (the famous gangster of the 1930s) was at when he was shot down by the FBI. We visited a few other places that had a little history just to take up time.

On our way back to the bus depot, we stopped at a mission called the History Center for Servicemen. While there visiting, we talked to the person in charge for a short time and looked around a bit. There was a stack of little black books of the New Testament, free to take. For some reason, I asked the clerk if I could have one. He grabbed one of the books, signed it, and gave to me, and then said, "God Speed." I thanked him and we all left. I'm not sure why I wanted the book, but something told me to take one. I think I was the only one in our group that did. I carried that book in my left breast pocket all the time I was in Korea.

After waiting well over three hours for our bus back to Hoptown (Hopkinsville, KY), we arrived back in camp late New Year's Eve and spent New Year's Day just lying around in the barracks. The next morning, we went back to our usual routine. At 4:00 A.M., the sergeant came through the barracks

45

yelling the same old thing, "Drop your c——s and grab your socks and report in formation in twenty minutes," sometimes more and sometimes less, depending on the situation. So we'd get up, take a shower and shave, and report in formation just outside the barracks, and go into our drills and calisthenics. The same old thing, but I loved it.

Through the remainder of the winter and into the spring, we continued with our drills, plus our tank training. We spent a lot of time on the range firing the big guns, going on maneuvers, and performing mock assaults supporting different infantry units; sometimes with the Airborne and sometimes with the 2nd Army Division.

During the training early that spring, I got promoted to staff sergeant. The position of tank driver called for the rank of SSgt., which I had been hoping for ever since I began to drive, and I was damn glad to finally get it. It helped a lot with the increase in my pay. My brother Kent and I now both had the rank of SSgt. I don't recall what Kent's MOS was, but by this time, I believe he was a tank commander and due for another promotion, which would be to sergeant first class (SFC).

Kent was living off base with his wife, Melba, at this time, so I didn't spend as much time with him as I had in the past. He was on and off base so much that as soon as drills or training were over for the day, he would leave to catch the bus and go home to where he lived in Clarksville, while I stayed on base all the time.

Early spring, we got our M46 Patton tanks with the 90 mm gun issued to us for training. We immediately started our training on them; we spent a lot of time on the firing range with the big gun, plus we did a lot of maintenance and servicing. We found out real soon the difference between the M4 Sherman tank and the M46 Patton. The M46 was a lot easier to handle. After we got well acquainted with the new tank, headquarters came out with a bulletin that Company A of the 141st would be named to carry out a new program called "Operation Miller." It was named after Capt. Richard Miller, former commander of Company B. He was selected to be the commanding officer of the program. Company A felt very honored to be the company chosen out of the 141st to participate in the project.

This project would go on for a period of three weeks and would be carried out entirely with crews from Company A. Why Company A was selected, no one ever said, but we all felt that it was quite an honor.

Our new M.46 Patton Tanks in formation

Our new M.46 Patton Tanks in formation

Our four-man tank crew left to right:
SFC Hale, Commander; Cpl. Tom Rivers, Gunner; SSgt. Dennis Ottley, Driver;
Name unknown, Loader

CHAPTER 6

"OPERATION MILLER"

So, when the orders came down from division headquarters, the 141st Tank Battalion was to go back in the field on an experimental program comparing the performance of a 4-man tank crew against a 5-man crew using the M46 Patton tanks with the 90 mm gun. The program was to include two platoons with five tanks each. Each tank crew, both 4-man and 5-man, would have an extra crew member as a supervisor, which would be a high ranking noncom. Their job would be to oversee the performance of each tank and tank crew that they were assigned to, and write up reports on the maintenance of the tank and the performance of the crew. The purpose of the program was to eventually cut tank crews from a 5-man crew to a 4-man crew, eliminating the assistant driver (bow-gunner), if it could be proven to be just as efficient.

This project was to last for a 3-week period out in the field. We were to bivouac all this time and chow would be brought out to us. We slept in our 2-man tents located near our tanks, and we were to keep our tanks in tiptop shape at all times.

I was assigned as driver on the first tank of the 4-man platoon. My commander would be SFC Jack Hale from Afton, WY, and my supervisor would be MSgt. Leland McCoy, also from Afton. It was my responsibility, as driver, to keep the tank clean and in good condition for operation purposes. This program was to last for three weeks in some of Camp Campbell's wettest and marshiest ground with a river nearby and, believe me, it proved to be some of the swampiest ground in the area. Within the first two weeks, every tank had gotten stuck, except ours. I don't know how we kept from getting stuck because we drove through the same marshes and areas that the rest of the tanks went through, but it did finally happen.

In the third week out, we finally got stuck in one hell of a hole in a very swampy area. We were really stuck. It took a lot to get us out. I guess I was walking pretty high for a while the first two weeks out, until I finally got stuck. Boy, did I get a razzing from the other drivers, but at least I could say I was the last. Every tank in the two platoons had gotten stuck during the project at least once, some twice. Both platoons spent a lot of time getting their tanks out of the marshes from where they were stuck.

Most of the time, when we got our tanks stuck during the three weeks, we had to use more than just another tank to get us out. Some of the time, we had to rig up a heavy chain with a winch and a block and tackle hooked on to what we called a dead-man. Sometimes, the dead man would be another tank, a big strong tree, or something that would hold and not give while the winch was working to pull the tank out. The way it worked was quite a system.

Also, while on this project, we practiced different tank formations and tactics. The one formation that we went into that was quite different from what we had done in the past was the old wagon train formation. We would drive our tanks into a circle like they used in the "Old West" against the Indians. They told us that this formation was being used in Korea to combat ground troops of the North Koreans and Chinese when they would attack tanks. The enemy would come at the tanks like a swarm of bees trying to damage and knock out the tanks the best way they possibly could. While this was happening, with the tank hatches buttoned up, each tank gunner and bog gunner would fire the .30-caliber machine guns that were mounted in the tanks at other tanks in the platoon, knocking off the enemy while they were swarming all over the tanks, knowing that machine gun fire could never pierce a tank. It seemed to work in practice, and I guess at one time or the other, they may have used it in Korea. We had heard that they had, but while we were in Korea, I don't recall it ever being used. But, that's what they told us and it could have been used in the early part of the war. It sounded reasonable.

Also, during Operation Miller, we had to unload all ammunition that the tank held, including all the 90 mm, the .30- and .50-caliber, plus all other small arms ammo. We also had to clean the big gun and remove, dismantle, and clean all movable tank weapons and small arms weapons, and completely clean and service the tank at least once during the 3-week period. Unloading that heavy ammo was not easy. We had to take it out of the floor of the turret, lay it all on a tarp on the ground, check it all out and, after cleaning the tank, put it all back. It was a couple days' chore.

We also drove our tanks in the river to wash them and bathe ourselves. We did a little swimming, cooling ourselves and having a lot of fun; we had a ball. It was so hot during this time it felt great to get in the water. They told

M.46 tanks stuck in the swamps during Operation Miller

M.46 tanks stuck in the swamps during Operation Miller

us to watch out for the water moccasin, but hell, after driving those tanks in the water, what moccasins were there would have been so scared that they probably ended up heading south someplace where it was safe, like in the Bayou or somewhere.

Over all, Operation Miller was a lot of fun and I believe we all learned a lot; I know I did. The M46 Patton tank proved to be a lot easier to drive than the M4 Sherman. It was faster, it had much more maneuverability, and it definitely gave more protection and fire power with the thicker armor and bigger gun. The army felt that it was a tank that would be equal to or even better than anything the enemy might have.

After Operation Miller was all over and all the scoring was in, and all the tallying was turned in to headquarters by the tank supervisors and others, it surprisingly turned out that the 4-man crew's performance proved to be just as efficient, or in some areas, even better than the 5-man crew had shown.

Although the 3-week project was a great learning period for the troops and a lot of fun, it did seem like a waste of time, mainly because it never changed a thing. As far as I know, the tanks still use the 5-man crew; I know they did throughout the Korean War. I guess the army just wanted to give us something to do; they were good at that.

One thing about the army, they seemed to be good at finding things for the troops to do, even if it was just a waste of time. It didn't matter; I guess it was part of the training. The other thing the army was good at was calling everybody out for something that you had to wait in line for, sometimes, for hours. The old army saying was, "Hurry up and wait," and that was only too true.

Now that Operation Miller was over and we were all back in the barracks, the first thing we did was grab a hot shower, and boy did it ever feel good. It also felt good to once again sleep between the sheets in our old army cots. Anyway, we were back in our barracks and everything was back to normal.

After we got through with Operation Miller, everybody that participated in the project got a 3-day pass. This was the end of May and all of my buddies were planning on a trip to New Orleans and wanted me to go, but my wife, Sandy, was too close to having our first baby, so I didn't dare leave the post. I missed out on the trip to New Orleans, but that was alright, I had other things on my mind.

So, I spent the next few days in the barracks and sometimes in the day room watching a snowy television. Most of the troops were on leave or lived off base, so it was a bit lonely. I did go down to the PX (Post Exchange) and bought a box of cigars to pass out when the baby was born, because I knew the troops would be after me for one.

SSgt. Dennis Ottley checking over 30 cal. machine gun

Tank and crew inspection: Left to right
Cpl. Tom Rivers, gunner; SFC Hale, Commander; MSgt. McCoy, Supervisor; loader
unknown and SSgt. Dennis Ottley, Driver

Ammo inspection: Left: Cpl. Marvin Treadway, Right: PFC Powers

SSgt. Dennis Ottley, Driver
checking and tightening up track sprocket

Crew active on Patton Tank, Left to Right:
Cpl. Tom Rivers and SSgt. Dennis Ottley

Left to Right: Cpl. Rivers and tank loafer, name unknown.

OPERATION MILLER
Washing tanks, doing our
laundrey and chowing down
"getting ready for final in-
spection"

M46 Patton	

USMC M46 in the Korean War.	
Type	Medium tank[1]
Place of origin	United States
Service history	
In service	1950 to mid-to-late-1950s
Wars	Korean War
Production history	
Manufacturer	Detroit Arsenal Tank Plant
Number built	800 + 360 M46A1
Variants	M46A1
Specifications	
Weight	48.5 tons (44 metric tons)
Length	27.82 ft (8.48 m)
Width	11.52 ft (3.51 m)
Height	10.43 ft (3.18 m)
Crew	5 (commander, gunner, loader, driver, assistant driver)

Medium Tank M4	

An M4A3E8 76 mm armed Sherman tank made during the Second World War	
Type	Medium tank
Place of origin	United States
Service history	
In service	1942–1955 (USA)
Used by	United States, and many others (see Foreign variants and use)
Wars	World War II, Greek Civil War, Arab-Israeli War, Korean War, Revolución Libertadora, Suez Crisis, Indo-Pakistani War of 1965, Six-Day War, Indo-Pakistani War of 1971, Yom Kippur War, 1958 Lebanon crisis, Lebanese Civil War, Cuban Revolution, Nicaraguan Revolution
Production history	
Designed	1940
Produced	1941–
Number built	49,234[1]
Specifications	
Weight	66,800 pounds (30.3 tonnes; 29.8 long tons; 33.4 short tons)
Length	19 ft 2 in (5.84 m)
Width	8 ft 7 in (2.62 m)
Height	9 ft (2.74 m)
Crew	5 (Commander, gunner, loader,

The morning of June 3, I got a call at headquarters that Sandy had gone into labor, so I was still just hanging out, waiting. Then later that night, I got another call from the folks that I was a proud papa of an eight and a half pound baby boy. He was born right at 8:30 P.M., Rocky Mountain Time, on June 3, 1951. Sandy's birthday was the next day, June 4, so, I called to wish her a "Happy Birthday" and talk to her about the baby. She sounded kind of down because she had quite a hard time. She said the baby was pretty bruised up because he was so big and had a tough time being born. She said kiddingly, "He looks so bad that if he doesn't get to looking better, he will probably have to depend on his personality because he sure won't be able to depend on his looks," but he turned out to be a pretty cute baby. We decided to name him Dennis Randell Ottley and call him Randy.

Now, I was the proud father of a bouncing baby boy, my first, and believe me that box of cigars went pretty fast after all the troops got back off their leave. I got a lot of razzing about being a father, but everyone seemed to be pretty happy for me. My buddies all said that they had a great time in New Orleans. I told them that I was sorry I missed it, but it was more exciting getting the word that I was now the father of a baby son.

My brother Kent and his wife, Melba, were also pretty happy for me. They had their firstborn, a little girl named Nikki, just about a month or so before. She was born on base at Camp Campbell.

CHAPTER 7

ON TO CAMP STONEMAN

By now it was mid-June when headquarters came out with a bulletin asking for volunteers to go to Korea. At this time, for some reason or other, they only wanted volunteers, which they had no problem getting. There was quite a bunch that volunteered from Company A, including some of my close buddies, SSgt. Jack Mathson, SSgt. Mike Lane, Cpl. Marvin Treadway, and SSgt. Bob Hillstead, all from Wyoming, plus a lot of others from our company and the battalion, mostly all single guys. They must have filled their quota because they never picked anyone else to go, only volunteers.

I thought about volunteering, but beings we just had our first baby, I didn't. Neither Sandy nor my mother wanted me to. After my best friend Paul Oaks got killed in Korea, my mother wasn't very happy about me even being in the service, let alone going into combat. She also had friends and people she knew that had been killed and wounded in WWII, so she definitely didn't want me to volunteer.

All the volunteers were scheduled to leave for Korea in mid-June, so Company A gave them kind of a send-off before they left, wishing them well and the best of luck. I hated to see them go, but I was sure they would be alright and would get a lot of experience by going to the Far East. I only hoped they would come back safe.

A month later in mid-July, headquarters called out a bunch more of the troops for Korean duty. This time, they never asked for volunteers, they just picked them. I was one of those picked and assigned to go. I don't know what criteria they used this time in their procedure of selecting, but they weren't looking for just volunteers this time. Plus, it didn't seem to matter whether you were married and had a family.

Others assigned to go from Wyoming out of Company A, besides myself, included SSgts. Boyd Henderson, Melvin Whitear, Ray Tanner, Verd Erickson, Ted Taylor, and two brothers, Robert (Bob) and William (Bill) Kimball, plus Cpls. Leonard Sims, Duane Drinkle, and James (Jim) Bateman. Also, there were three others from Wyoming out of Company B that were picked to go, SSgt. Robert (Bob) Logan, SSgt. Donald Brown, and Cpl. Virgil Overy. In addition, they also assigned quite a few of the new young recruits from the South to go.

The Army's purpose for assigning so many troops out of the 141st Tank Battalion at this particular time was to replace all-black units. The 24th Infantry Regiment was an all-black (Negro) unit, sometimes called the "the Deuce-Four" of the 25th Infantry Division. Those from the 141st Tank Battalion that were selected to go would be replacing all the black troops in the Tank Company of the 24th and other all-black tank units.

•   •   •

In 1948, President Harry S. Truman signed an executive order that he intended to desegregate all-black units in the military. When the Korean War began in June 1950, black service personal in the Army were still assigned to racially segregated units. In such units, all of the soldiers, including the non-commissioned officers were black, as were some of the lieutenants and captains, but almost all the senior officers were white. Years ago in 1950, the descriptive term for black people was Negro or colored. The term black is a more recent designation.

The largest all-black unit was the 24th Infantry Regiment of the 25th Infantry Division nicknamed "the Deuce-Four," which was stationed at Gifu in Japan when the war began. The desegregation actually started in early 1951 when black soldiers began to be assigned to previously all-white units. Of the estimated 33,629 American troops killed in combat during the Korean War, 3,223 or 9.3% were black.

•   •   •

Not knowing why I was one of the troops selected to go, I was kind of glad that I was. During WWII, I had hoped to have a chance to join the service so I could help out in the war, but I was only 13 years of age when it ended, so I didn't make it. Well, it seemed that I was going to get my chance now, because it looked like I was heading for Korea to help fight a war.

There was never another assignment of troops to be selected for Korean duty after we were picked from the 141st. My brother Kent never got called for overseas duty. He was to stay with the 141ˢᵗ Tank Battalion as one of the training personnel. Kent was a good soldier and would do a great job in training new troops.

A few months after we left, the 141ˢᵗ Tank Battalion became cadre, a training outfit. They were transferred to Fort Ord, CA, to train new recruits. Fort Ord was a training center for new personnel, and the 141ˢᵗ had been sent there to train them to be tankers.

The best thing about being selected for Korean duty was that we got a 10-day leave before going over. I was scheduled for a furlough anyway, but I was pretty happy to be going home, even if it was for just 10 days. When we were all ready to leave Camp Campbell, some of us made a deal with SSgt. Bob Kimball to ride with him in his pickup, and help pay for the gas and any other expenses. We thought that would be a lot less expensive than taking a train or bus. None of us had a whole lot of money, so we were looking at the cheapest way to get home, even though most of the time we would be riding in the back of the truck.

Bob Kimball's wife, Norma, was also there and was going with us. There was only room for one of us to sit in the front with Bob and his wife, so all the way home the guys in the back would trade off to give each of us a little rest from the hard bed of the truck. Bob and his wife sat in the cab all the way, with Bob driving.

Besides me, going with Bob Kimball was his brother Bill, Boyd Henderson, Jim Bateman, Duane Drinkle, and Ray Tanner. We left the camp early in the morning so we got to Evanston late that night. We never stopped, only to gas up and grab something to eat. It was quite a rough trip and we were all damn glad to get home. We had to stop in Bridger Valley to let Tanner off. His ranch was just outside of Mountain View.

It was late when we got home, but I had finally got to meet my son Randy. I thought he was pretty cute; all his bruises and marks from being born had disappeared. He seemed to be a good and a happy baby, always laughing and grinning, not crying much. But, I was really happy to be home to be with my wife and baby, and seeing my mother and all.

The thing about getting a furlough at this time, I got to be home on July 26, our first wedding anniversary. It was also my sister's and her husband's anniversary. We both got married on the July 26, but different years. So, on our anniversary and while I was home, we got together and decided to go to the Saltair Resort located at the Great Salt Lake in Utah—Sandy and I with our baby Randy; my sister and her husband, Johnny, and their two children Lynn and Shelley, all went. We had a great time.

Saltair was an amusement park with a large dance hall, a roller coaster, and a lot of other different rides. At this time, it was the largest amusement park in Utah and was known to have had the largest roller coaster in the country. There was also a lot of swimming off the beach. However, with the lake being so heavy with salt, a person didn't really do too much swimming, mostly just floating and getting a suntan, and sometimes a sunburn. It was a popular place for people to go at the time, but several years later, when the roller coaster had burned down; they closed it up and never opened their amusement park again.

While Sandy and I rode the roller coaster, the wind blew my garrison cap off my head; I never did find it. It could have blown just about anywhere. The rest of the day, I was without my cap, hoping an MP wouldn't be around to question me why I wasn't in full uniform, but I did get back to Evanston with no problems. I had another cap in my duffle bag at home. Other than losing my cap, it was a great day. I got to enjoy a day with my sister and brother-in-law and their kids, but most of all, with my wife and baby.

While on furlough, we also went out to Pete's Rock-N-Rye and other places dancing, drinking, and enjoying ourselves. It was an enjoyable ten days, but it was coming to an end. We were all scheduled to report in at Camp Stoneman, CA, on August 4 for orientation for overseas duty. Boyd Henderson, Jim Bateman, Ray Tanner, and I were scheduled to catch the Greyhound bus out of Evanston on August 3 for Camp Stoneman.

While waiting for the bus, Sandy and I spent a few minutes visiting with her folks and some friends in the City Bar next to the bus stop. The folks were with their friends, Wayne and Mabel Owens, among others. Before we left, Wayne bought a fifth of Seagram's VO and gave it to me. He said that he was really proud of us and wanted to thank all of us for serving the country and to have a good trip and stay safe.

While on the bus heading to Stoneman, we opened the bottle of Seagram's and had a few snorts out of it before we got to camp, but we got there with no problems and reported for duty first thing the morning of August 4. As we entered the gate at Stoneman, we noticed a sign that read, THROUGH THESE PORTALS PASS THE BEST DAMN SOLDIERS IN THE WORLD. This inscription made me feel proud and as if I was there for a real and worthwhile purpose.

Camp Stoneman was located near Pittsburg, CA, in the East Bay region of the San Francisco Bay area. It served as a major staging area for the Army during both WWII and the Korean War. It was the entrance for our trip to Korea. After we got to Stoneman, we were told to go to a hall about the size of a gym. The area was nothing but wall-to-wall soldiers with their duffle bags.

While there, we got some instructions on what to expect on our trip across the Pacific and that we would be stopping at Camp Drake in Japan before continuing to Korea. The next two days we went through more orientation. Also,

At the Saltaire
Left to right: my niece, Shelley; my sister, Terry;
her husband, Johnny, my nephew, Lynn;
and myself holding my baby, Randy
and my wife, Sandy

Camp Stoneman

Though the sound of thousands of marching feet is but a memory today, not so very long ago Camp Stoneman was the principal "jumping off point" for more than one million American soldiers destined for military operations in the Second World War's Pacific Theater, and again several years later during the Korean War. Consisting of more than 2,500 sprawling acres, Camp Stoneman sprang to life near the town of Pittsburg in 1942 to as the San Francisco Port of Embarkation's primary troop staging center. The function of the post was to receive and rapidly process troops for overseas service by completing paperwork and updating records, arranging for last minute training, providing medical and dental care, and issuing and servicing equipment.

The USNS Gen. Wm. Weigel: the transport ship that we sailed on from Camp Stoneman (San Francisco Bay area) to Korea.

USNS Gen. Wm. Weigel on its way heading out to see for Korea.

while at Stoneman, we received a few shots in the arm. I don't recall what the shots were for, but it had something to do with keeping us immune from certain diseases. Plus, we had the usual physical examinations, such as the "short-arm" and the one where they tell you to assume the position, grab the ankles, and "spread the cheeks."

It seemed like that was the "army way," to tell us to hurry up, but when we got there, it seemed like we always had to stand in line for an hour or two, waiting. We stood in line a lot of the time while in the service. One of the army's famous sayings was "hurry up and wait." That was so true.

After a few days at Stoneman, we were ready to ship out. Early that morning, we loaded up in trucks, heading for the docks with our duffle bags. When we got to the docks to load up, I saw the biggest ship I had ever seen. It was a troop ship that transported military personnel to the Far East. The name on the ship was *USS General William Weigel.*

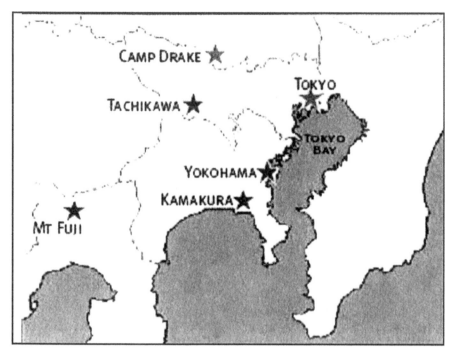

Map of Tokyo Bay, Japan, and area...

Barracks at Camp Drake

CHAPTER 8

ACROSS THE PACIFIC

The *USS General Weigel* was one of the Navy's largest ships that they used at the time to transport US troops for duty in Korea. It would carry almost 5,000 troops, plus the crew, and traveled at a speed up to 21 knots. I looked at the ship and thought to myself *so this is the ship that is going to carry us across the Pacific to Korea. Boy, this is going to be some kind of an experience, going across the big ocean*, and it did turn out to be quite an adventure.

That morning, we all unloaded from the trucks and fell in formation. The sergeant in charge started calling our names out alphabetically, and as our name was called, we were to start walking up the ramp to board the ship. When I got on board and was looking at the deck and the size of the area on board, it was quite amazing.

As we got on board, they directed us to an area below deck where we would bunk. The area was nothing but wall-to-wall bunks, four or five deep. So, by the time all the troops got on board, it was pretty damn crowded, especially down where everyone bunked, but we all knew that we were there for the next two or three weeks, so we had just better learn to like it and do the best we could.

As we boarded the ship, I got separated from Boyd Henderson, Ray Tanner, and some of the others from the 141st Tank Battalion, but it didn't take long before we found each other and got together again. It was nice to be with someone you knew on board, but it didn't take long to get to know others. All the troops I got acquainted with seemed to be great guys, and I got to know quite a few.

As we left the San Francisco Bay area, we sailed under the Golden Gate Bridge and headed out to sea. Sailing under the bridge was quite a sight, but what was to come was going to be even more so. I just wondered how long it was going to be before I got sea sick, because some of the troops got sick on the first day out.

It happened on the third day out when I finally got sea sick. On that particular day, I had gone down to the latrine; what a mess. When I got there, it was full of GIs, most of them sea sick and heaving their guts out. Between the horrible smell from the troops throwing up and some taking a crap, plus being excessively hot, I also got sea sick, and it hit me like a ton of bricks. At that time, I joined the rest of them, heaving and throwing up, but that was the only time I got sick during the entire trip. The rest of the voyage I felt really good and actually ended up enjoying myself.

It was a great experience for me and something completely new. There were a few things that weren't too enjoyable about the trip. One was the close quarters where we bunked. I don't recall for sure, but the bunks were either 4 deep or 5 deep and there was not much room between them. It was pretty crowded, but then what can you expect when you have almost 5,000 troops aboard?

I don't think any of us cared for the chow served on the ship. For breakfast, it seemed like we had scrambled eggs an awful lot of the time. Sometimes we had hot cakes and other food, but the scrambled eggs were served more often, or maybe it just seemed like it because we had them so much of the time, and believe me, they tasted terrible. I had never seen or eaten green eggs like this before. They told us that the eggs were powdered and when scrambled, they turned out to be green in color. They looked awful and tasted just as bad. The food was bad, but the eggs alone would have made you sick.

For dinner, it seemed like we had SOS (Shit on a Shingle) a lot of the time. At first, it didn't taste too bad, but when you got it as often as we did, after a while it didn't taste good, at all. I don't know what the crew of the ship had for their meals, but if it was the same, I was damn glad I was in the army and not the navy. But, I think they had their own mess hall and probably had pretty good meals, because in my experience so far, we had had pretty good chow in the army. What we would get in Korea, we would just have to wait and see.

Another thing bad about the trip was not being able to shower in fresh water all the time. The first several days out we had fresh water, but the last part of the trip we had to shower in salt water. When you shower in salt water, you and your hair end up being really sticky, so I only showered once the last week we were on the trip. After my first experience showering with salt water, I wasn't about to take one again.

The weather was good during the entire trip with clear skies and smooth sailing. This made the voyage much more enjoyable. I spent a good share of my time up on the deck near the stern, watching the dolphins, the flying fish, and the birds. There was always some kind of ocean life following the ship because of the wet garbage it left behind.

I also enjoyed watching the wake that was caused by the ship's movement. It was beautiful on clear nights, especially when the moon was out. It had a bluish color of many shades, sparkling and glistering from the movement of the ship and the moonlight leaving a beautiful sight. It was fun to watch. As long as I stayed top side in the fresh air and had the cool ocean breeze blowing on me, I felt pretty good, but when I had to go down to the latrine, I seemed to always feel a little sick, but I was able to overcome it.

There wasn't really much to do on the trip so a good share of the time I would either read a book or do a little gambling by playing poker or blackjack. I never won much in poker, but I did pretty well playing blackjack. As a non-com, I got called out to oversee work details a few times, mostly to clean up an area, or paint something that really didn't need it, but the military had a way of keeping everyone busy, one way or the other. The army always told us, "It don't matter whether you're busy or not, just always look busy," and if you didn't, they would make damn sure you were. They could always find something to keep you busy, even if it wasn't necessary or needed.

After about eight or nine days out of Camp Stoneman, we crossed the International Date Line, losing a day. It had never crossed my mind that I would ever see the day that I would be crossing such a line, but it was something else that I learned that when going west you lost a day and going east you gained a day...kind of exciting.

About the thirteenth day, we were getting close to Japan and started entering the Japanese waters. We noticed there were a lot of small boats in the area. We were told that most of them were fishing for whales and were called whalers. As we approached the island of Japan, we happened to see one of the whalers hook a whale, but after a while, the action moved out of sight. We never did know what the outcome was, but it was fun watching them for a few minutes. We heard from the ship's crew that whale fishing was a large industry in Japan.

•   •   •

Throughout the Korean conflict, the United States and some of the United Nations' forces were fortunate to have Japan as a forward base to the Far East. Japan's ports and facilities, plus the hard-working people of Japan, were a real asset in keeping the operating forces well-supplied and repaired, as well as providing relaxation and recreation for naval and military personnel.

• • •

The morning of the fourteenth day we landed in Japan by way of Tokyo Bay. We were to spend a few days at Camp Drake before continuing on to Korea. Camp Drake was located about 30 miles northwest of Tokyo. It was one of about twenty military installations around the Tokyo area at that time, and was used often for a stopping point for GIs bound for Korea.

Before all of us left the ship, some of the NCOs (non-commissioned officers) were left there to be in charge of some details to clean up the latrines, the bunk quarters, and other areas that needed cleaning up. I was one of those NCOs. We didn't get to leave the ship until the ship was cleaned up and in "ship shape," as they would say. Most of the troops had already left.

After leaving the ship, we were bused to the camp and taken to the barracks where they assigned bunks to us. We would be spending a few days at Camp Drake, going through more inspections, short-arm, etc., and a whole lot of orientation concerning our tour in Korea.

During these orientations, they not only told us about the sub-zero weather in the wintertime and the sizzling hot summers in the summertime, but they also told us what to expect while in combat and what kind of enemy we were up against. Some of the information they gave us stuck with me, and all the time during my tour in Korea, I thought about it.

They told us, "If you ever get into a situation where you are captured, do everything you can to escape." They claimed that both the North Koreans and the Chinese hated tankers so much that if you were captured, they would put you through a lot of torture, the kind of torture that you wouldn't wish on anyone. I don't know whether that was true or not, but I'm sure some of the things they told us were for our own good and to let us know what we were to expect and possibly run up against.

Other things they told us that stuck in my mind were about some of the dangers that we had to look out for not related to combat. One was be careful and watch out for the little viper snakes in Korea. They said they were very poisonous and could either paralyze you or kill you. I guess they were dangerous, especially in the summertime. I never saw one during my time over there, but I guess a lot of the troops saw them, especially the infantry. I don't recall the actual name for them. The other thing they informed us about was the rats in Korea. They said that we could find them anywhere in the country. They told us that these rats carry a disease that can be fatal, and if it didn't kill you, it would make you damn sick. The disease was some kind of virus that some called the "Manchurian Fever." Some called it the "Hemorrhagic Fever."

They also said, "Whatever you do, don't shoot them or use them for target practice; the fleas and lice on them is what causes the fever, not the bite." They told us not to ever touch a dead rat without gloves and be very careful even then. They indicated that if you were to shoot one with your .45 automatic, it would blow that rat all over the place and make it more dangerous than ever. So, they warned us not to use them for target practice.

They said that when you get to your destination in Korea, the army would make available a rat poison that looked like moth balls, and would instruct us to spread them around our tents and bunkers. Apparently, the rats would eat the poison and then wander off somewhere else and die.

Some of the guys in our outfit didn't listen too closely to the advice, because there were some, being stupid, that did use them for target practice. There were a couple of GIs in our tank company sent home with the disease. It was mostly because they got careless with their food, leaving it out where the rats could get to it. I'm not sure whether they lived or died, I never did hear; but I do know that they were damn sick when they left. We had been informed that there had been quite a few troops throughout the war that ended up going home because of the disease from the rats. Getting it was a sure way of going home. Some went very sick and some went in coffins, mostly from being careless with their food and not listening to good advice. As we were told, we always kept our food in metal containers like an ammo box or something metal.

After three days at Camp Drake, we were bused back to the Tokyo docks and boarded the same ship, the USS *General William Weigel*. After embarking, we sailed back out to the Pacific Ocean from Tokyo Bay, going around Japan, we entered the Yellow Sea. For four days, we traveled from Japan to Korea. We reached Inchon, Korea, early the morning of August 31, 1951, with all of us wondering what was to happen next, and where do we go from here. That morning, we would probably have all the answers, at least, we all hoped to.

As we arrived in the harbor at Inchon, we noticed that the harbor was loaded with ships from all other United Nations countries that were there to assist the South Koreans in their fight for freedom. It was quite a sight.

As we got closer to Inchon, I noticed the water was awfully dirty in that particular area. I had never seen water that dirty anywhere else during our voyage; it looked filthy. I know I wouldn't have wanted to go swimming in that area. I also noticed that there was an awful odor in the air and as we got closer, it got stronger. I was told it was coming from the land. They said that the Koreans used human waste for fertilizing their rice patties. I suppose that was where most of the smell was coming from. We found out later that the Koreans used buckets to carry human waste in, buckets that the GIs always referred to as "honey buckets." Sometimes, they would also use the buckets filled with vegetables that they would bury for a long time for later use. After digging them up, the vegetables would turn rotten and have an awful odor that if close by, would even choke a horse. I think they used the rotten veggies for fertilizer also, but hell, for all I knew they might have eaten them. The way they lived, starving half the time, I wouldn't have been surprised or I wouldn't have blamed them a bit.

That morning we disembarked from the ship by the rope ladders on the side with all our gear and equipment to the landing barges that were actually called LCVP (Landing Craft Vehicle Personnel) vehicles. When we got to shore, we were now in South Korea, known as "the Land of the Morning Calm." They marched us to an area where we were told we could take a shower, and that we had to shower before chow. We entered a building where we had to strip down butt-naked. That was okay, but the problem was the showers were outside in an open area, which was fenced.

After stripping down, I stepped out of the building stark naked, and the first thing I noticed was a big crowd of Korean people—men, women, and children—standing outside the fence (it was a strong wire fence). They were laughing and pointing at all the GIs showering. It looked like they were pointing and laughing at their private parts; anyway, whatever it was, they were getting a big bang out of the whole thing.

At first, I was too embarrassed to go out and had second thoughts about even taking a shower, but I knew I had to. They said, "No shower, no chow." There was no way of getting out of it, so I thought *what the hell* and went for it, embarrassed or not. It was another time to remember, another moment I would never forget.

So, I jumped in the shower, and boy did it ever feel good. After being on the ship all that time, I needed a fresh water shower and it was such a hot summer day—100 degrees plus—I knew it would feel good and it did. It felt so good, I forgot about the audience and their carrying on, and I enjoyed the shower. It was quite an experience for all of us.

Afterwards, we went to a mess hall to eat. The breakfast was pretty good, much better than what we had on the ship. When we were finished with chow, they lined us up in formation and marched us to an area where army trucks were lined up waiting for us. We loaded up into the trucks and headed east for Seoul. As we drove through Inchon, looking around, we noticed that most of the buildings and areas had been severely damaged and badly beaten up. It looked like they may have had an earthquake or something, but it was the war. The entire area looked very devastated. It was a sight that a person would never forget and made you wonder how the Korean people ever survived it.

76

As we rode through Inchon and on the road to Seoul, you couldn't help but notice the destruction caused by the war, and how sad the people appeared. It made you think how fortunate we Americans were and why we were there. These people had been pushed back and forth from South Korea to North Korea in extreme heat and in freezing cold. Many of them had been on foot in the worst weather conditions of heat, rain, mud, and freezing snow. You might say that they had been through hell. A lot of them lost family members by either being misplaced or through death, plus some lost their homes and property. They had to be tough to endure what they had gone through. You had to feel sorry for them, but at the same time, you had to admire them.

The Soldier's Creed

I am an American Soldier.
I am a warrior and a member of a Team.
I serve the People of the United States and live the Army values.
I will always place the mission first.
I will never accept defeat.
I will never quit.
I will never leave a fallen comrade.
I am disciplined, physically and mentally tough,
Trained and proficient in my warrior tasks and drills.
I always maintain my arms, my equipment, and myself.
I am an expert and I am a professional.
I stand ready to deploy, engage, and destroy, the enemies of the
United States of America in close combat.
I am a guardian of freedom and the American way of life.
I am an American Soldier.

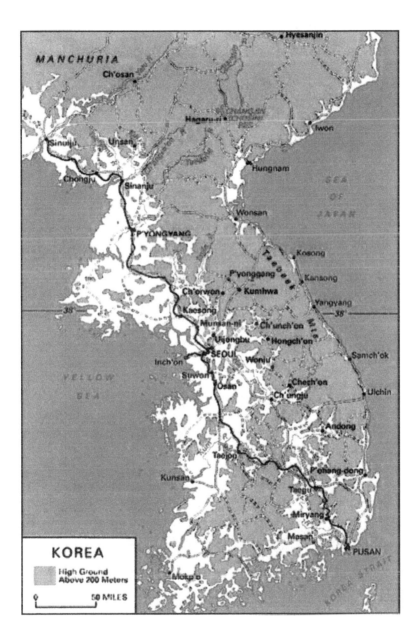

KOREA

High Ground
Above 200 Meters

0   50 MILES

CHAPTER 9

PASSING THROUGH SEOUL

During our ride from Inchon, we also noticed that there were a lot of rice paddies along the way. We were told that rice paddies were all over South Korea and that rice was their largest industry of produce and export. They also said that the rice paddies made it more difficult for tanks to maneuver and get around because of so many of them.

Rice paddies were deep in water for irrigation purposes, making the ground under them very marshy. This made it tough for tanks to maneuver in Korea, especially South Korea where most of the farming was done. When a tank or any vehicle got into a paddy, it could be well stuck and would be made very vulnerable to the enemy. Tankers tried very hard to avoid the paddies. This made it even tougher for them to be as effective as they could have been if Korea hadn't had so many rice paddies. Tankers tried to stay on dry roads and dry ground as much as possible.

As we approached the capital city of Seoul, we noticed more damage and destruction from the war. Seoul had been hit pretty badly. We noticed one building that had only one wall standing. All the buildings seemed to have some kind of damage, but a lot of them were completely destroyed to where all that was left was a pile of rubble. We also noticed residential areas that had been damaged.

As we continued through the area heading for the military headquarters, we noticed the Korean people stop and stare at us as if they were wondering why we were there, but I'm sure they knew why. It was hard to read what was on their minds or how they felt. All they did was look at us and stare. I suppose they were used to seeing American troops coming through. Most of the kids looked like a bunch of orphans, and many of them were. You couldn't help feeling sorry for them, but it did make us wonder just what the hell we were doing there.

After being in Korea for a while, understanding the people more and knowing what they had gone through, plus what they were up against, we understood more of why we were there, and after understanding the South Koreans' situation we had a better feeling about it. For the most part, I believe most GIs felt pretty good about being there. These people had gone through hell and deserved to be free. Like I said, you couldn't help feeling bad for them. Plus, after being around them for a while, we found that they were people with a great sense of humor. They were very friendly and laughed at most everything.

When the North Koreans crossed the 38th Parallel, they immediately overpowered the South Koreans without much trouble mainly because of the ROK (Republic of Korea), the South Korean army, did not have the manpower or the equipment to hold them back. The South was a beaten nation at that point until the United States and their allies entered the conflict in July 1950.

While in Seoul, we received our orders of what outfit we would be assigned to, what division and regiment, plus what our position would be. If I remember right, we also had to turn all our American currency in for military script while in Seoul. It was kind of hard to give up our American dollars for a bunch of paper money that looked like Monopoly money. Some of the troops, trying to be funny, made smart-ass remarks about it. I remember one guy smarting off and saying, "What the hell are we doing playing games, or are we going to fight a war?" The troops just kind of snickered; the sergeant in charge gave him a dirty look, but didn't say anything. I suppose they were used to it.

Military script was only paper money, no coins. As I remember, the script started with five cents and went only as high as a twenty dollar bill, all paper. If there was anything bigger than a twenty, I'd never seen it. Hell, I was happy to have a twenty.

After being in Korea for a while, some of us ended up with some real Korean money, but it wasn't worth much. The only Korean money I ended up with was a 1,000 won, and I don't believe it was worth more than ten cents in American money. I don't recall just how the Korean money compared with the American dollar at that time, but I know it wasn't worth near as much.

As far as our assignments went, most of the transfers from the 141st Tank Battalion were assigned to the Tank Company of the 14th Infantry Regiment and would be attached to the 25th Infantry Division, replacing the all-black unit, the 24th Infantry Regiment (the Deuce-Four). I was assigned as a tank driver, as I hoped I would be. That was my MOS (Military Occupational Specialty) when I left the states; I loved driving those tanks. Most of the transfers

SEOUL, KOREA
August 1951
Ruins from
the war
Note:
Bottom photo
with just the
front wall
standing.

Fish market in Seoul's downtown business district.

Elderly Korean man (Papa-san) carrying a loaded "A" frame.

Korean folks shopping in Seoul's downtown business distrcit

Typical residential area of Seoul.

Young Korean boy (boy-san) standing near his home in Seoul.

Young Korean girl (girl-san) near ruins in business district.

*Photos
of young
Korean children
(some orphans)
on the streets
of Seoul.*

Photo of a religious temple in Seoul, Korea.
Apparently it was never harmed by the war.

Photo of the building in Seoul used by Americans and allies,
also used as a rest home for GI's.

from Wyoming were among those assigned to the tank company, putting me in the same outfit as some of my buddies from Wyoming.

After going through more orientation on why we were there and what to expect, plus a little malarkey, we loaded up in the trucks again and headed north toward the 38th Parallel. As we moved north, we met a lot of troops heading south. At this time, we had no idea where we were going. We knew we were heading toward the front, but didn't know just where.

After we crossed the 38th, we set up bivouac in an area about fifteen miles into North Korea. This was to be a temporary stopover lasting just a few days. Our instructions were to setup our 2-man tents, that we would be spending the next two or three days at this location. It had been a long day since we left the ship and we were all pretty tired, so we were all looking forward to having chow and then just relaxing for a while and getting a good night's sleep, but were we ever fooled.

They instructed us, before chow and before settling down, that each tent was to dig a foxhole about 3 to 4 feet long and at least arm-pit deep near each tent. We asked them why, but as usual, they just said, "Don't ask why, just do it." I guess they just wanted to give us something to do, or just maybe they were preparing us for the possibility of an attack. No one argued, we just did it and figured that the ones in charge knew what they were doing. We hoped it wouldn't be an attack or something because we hadn't even been armed, yet. Then they came up with a roster for guard duty. Guard duty would be for one hour and then relieved. I didn't get it until the next night.

Finally, the mess truck had arrived and we all settled down for chow using our mess gear for the first time. After digging the trenches we were all tired and damn hungry. We were ready for chow and a rest.

While we were camped there, we found out real soon that the Korean people were always referred to as something-*san*. For instance, adult Koreans were referred to as *Papa-san* for adult man and *Mama-san* for an adult woman, a young boy was *boy-san*, and a young girl was *baby-san*. That's the way we would call them to get their attention, with such as terms like *e-dee-wha* (meaning "come here"), or *kuda* (meaning "scram"), and so on.

Other terms of military slang and phonetically sounded words commonly used by GIs in Korea were:

ah-ri-ga-to	thank you	*bera bera* talk	too much
chin-gu	friend	*chon-gee*	stop, halt
chop chop	hurry up, food, eat	*cho-sum-nee-dah*	okay, all right
cho-ah-mah-tay	wait a minute	*dai-jo-be*	understand, okay
Gook	North Korean (enemy)	*hew-gee*	toilet paper

honcho	leader, boss	*ichi-ban*	number one, the best
kemo sabe	friend	*ko-ni-chi-wha*	good afternoon
mosh-skosh	do it quick	*muul*	water
mush-ee-dah	drink	*neh*	yes
oh-ka-nay	money	*oh-sheep-she-oh*	welcome
slicky boy	thief, butterfly boy	*su-ko-shi*	few, a little bit
sy-o-nara	goodbye	*tak-son*	much, many
um-sheek	food	*watashi*	I, myself

CHAPTER 10

A DARK NIGHT, A WOUNDED SOLDIER

SFC Boyd Henderson from Evanston and I shared the tent together, and after we got through with chow, we went to our tent to try to get some rest. They told us to sleep with all our clothes on, except our boots. Wondering why, they said, "You might just as well get used to it; you'll be sleeping fully clothed most of the time when you get to the front, anyway."

By the time dark of night came, all the troops, except those picked for the first hour of guard duty, had already gone to sleep. It really felt good to finally be able to stretch out and get some rest; it had been a long day. However, our respite didn't last long; all of a sudden, something woke us up.

It happened to be a very dark night, and after we had gotten to sleep with all our clothes on, except for our boots, about 10:00 P.M., a loud blast woke us up. Someone hollered out, "Up and at 'em. Get out of your tents fast and into the foxholes! This is an alert!" We grabbed our boots and left the tent for our foxhole.

As Henderson and I waited in our foxhole, trying to put our boots on, all of a sudden we heard an airplane flying over, but couldn't see it. Pretty soon, a guy's voice came over a loud speaker saying things such as, "Go home, GI, go home! Go home to your loved ones; you have no business over here," he went on and on, telling us to go home and why we shouldn't be there. The guy spoke such good English, we couldn't tell just what nationality he was. As far as we were concerned, he might have been American. It was hard to tell. It seemed like the plane was flying around for about 15 to 20 minutes with the voice saying the same thing over and over again. We could hear the plane, but couldn't see it; it had no lights, plus it was a very dark night.

After the plane left, we got orders to leave our foxholes and meet with everyone to find out what had just happened. Those in charge told us that had been who the North Koreans called "Chinaman Charley," sometimes called "Goodtime Charley," or "Bedcheck Charley," and that they would first drop a bomb, not wanting to hit anything in particular, but to wake you up. Then the plane would fly around above us, high enough where you couldn't see it, talking on a loud speaker with a bunch of propaganda, hoping you would get the message and go home or surrender to their side. They said that they seemed to always pick a very dark night.

The next morning, reveille was called, telling us to "rise and shine, we got things to do." Putting our boots back on and leaving our tent, it appeared like it was going to be another hot day, and it was—100 degrees plus. The mess truck arrived, we grabbed our mess gear, and after going through another line, we chowed down for breakfast, which wasn't too bad. Matter of fact, it was really quite tasty.

After chow, they told us that today we would be issued our sidearm, the .45-caliber automatic pistol with the holster and the ammunition for it. They said it was alright to load the clip, but do not put a shell in the chamber at this time. Some didn't listen.

That afternoon, we were all showing off our .45s, talking and mingling around, feeling pretty good now that we were finally armed, when all of a sudden, everything went wrong. There was a shot fired by one of our own GIs, wounding another.

What happened was one of the soldiers had handed his pistol to a buddy to look at. Not knowing there was a shell in the chamber, which everyone was told not to do at this time, his buddy pulled the trigger and the round hit the GI in the gut. He was shot by his own gun. When he was hit, the force of the shot spun him around and dropped him to the ground immediately. It appeared to be a very serious gut wound. He appeared to be bleeding pretty badly, until someone grabbed his first aid packet and dressed his wound as best he could until a medic got there.

The medic immediately called for a helicopter, which landed nearby several minutes later. The wounded soldier was still alive and appeared to be doing pretty well when they loaded him in the helicopter. He was taken to the MASH (Mobile Army Surgical Hospital) unit for treatment. After that, I never heard any more about him, whether he lived or not, but either way he would have been sent home.

The soldiers involved had both been from the 141st Tank Battalion in the states and both from Georgia. I don't recall the name of the one that got shot, but the one that shot him accidentally was a PFC Powers. I remember it took him a long time to get over it. We all felt bad for both of them. It was kind of ironic, being our first wounded, and that it happened at the hand of one of our own and not the enemy. It kind of ruined the whole day for all of us.

That night, I drew guard duty for the first hour. It was a dark night and kind of spooky, but there were no more problems.

The next morning, we all assembled for reveille and then we were told that we would be leaving the area after chow, and that we would not be riding in trucks, we would be hoofing it. Tankers on foot, boy that should get some laughs, and it did.

After falling into formation with full pack, roll call was taken. Ready and waiting to move out, they told us we would be going on foot for a few miles to an area near Kumhwa. Our location would be close to the front lines known as the MLR (Main Line of Resistance). We would also be in an area called the "Iron Triangle."

The so-called Iron Triangle was a triangular shaped area of relatively flat terrain with a few hills about 30 miles north of the 38th Parallel in east-central North Korea. The village of Kumhwa was at the eastern base and the village of Chorwon was at the western base. At the northern apex was the village of Pyonggang (not to be confused with the North Korean capital of Pyongyang). The region included rail lines and highways running to the Manchurian border, and it was very essential that this area be held by the Allies.

So, we started hoofing it down the dirt road, heading farther north into North Korea. On our way, we had several military trucks pass us also going north, mostly loaded with infantry. Just as we expected, we did get harassed, teased, and laughed at because we were on foot and they were riding, when normally we would be riding and they would be on foot. They hollered out things like, "Hey, tanker, where's your tank?" or "Hey, cavalry, where's your horse?" because tankers were the modern day cavalry, and then they would laugh like hell. Most of us laughed with them; some guys flipped them off, but it was all in fun.

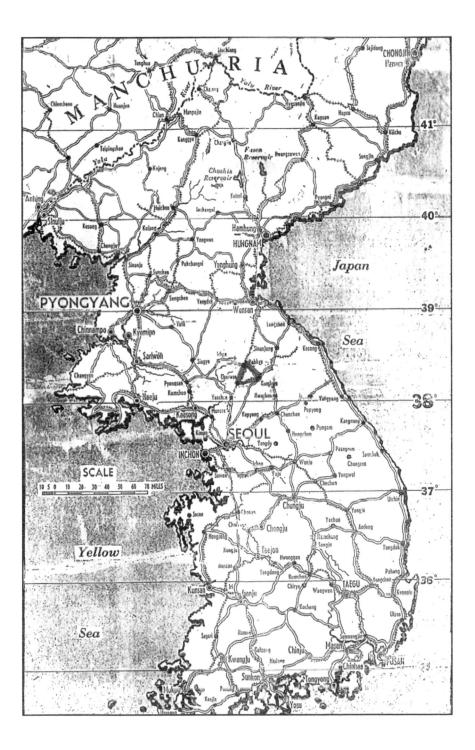

CHAPTER 11

IRON TRIANGLE

With tired feet and a lot of bitching, we finally reached our reserve area. If I remember right, our tanks had already arrived. After setting up our squad tents and preparing other necessities, such as headquarters, the mess tent, the supply tent, etc., we also had to prepare a place for the latrine. After we were set up, we got to chow down and then relax the rest of the evening. We were now officially the Tank Company of the 14th Infantry Regiment, 25th Infantry Division.

· · ·

14th Infantry Regiment – Golden Dragons

As the Civil War loomed, the 14th Infantry Regiment was organized in 1861 as part of the expansion of the Regular Army. The 14th went on to compile a truly distinguished record during the Civil War. It's ranking Captain Paddy O'Connell, who once said, "I would take the 14th to the very gates of Hell, but I want the chance to whip the Devil when I get there," often led the 14th into battle.

When asked where the 14th should be placed in the Grand Review celebrating the Union victory, General George Meade, commander of the Army of the Potomac said, "To the right of the line. The 14th has always been to the front in battle and deserves the place of honor."

From that statement, the 14th later adopted the slogan, "The Right of the Line."

After the Civil War, the 14th was sent west to the Presidio of San Francisco in 1865 because of the warring Indian nations and white lawlessness. From there, they were sent out to stations in Arizona, California, Oregon, and Washington.

Later in the 1870s the 14th participated in the Indian problems in the Dakota Territory. For its service in the Indian Wars and the West, the regiment received participation credit for four campaigns: Little Big Horn, Bannocks, Arizona 1866, and Wyoming 1874.

With the declaration of war with Spain, the 14th was ordered to the Philippines in July 1898. In 1900, they fought in the Boxer Rebellion in China, and were later sent back to Manila to guard warehouses and offices. In 1901, they received orders to return to the states.

Upon the entrance of the United States into World War I in 1917, the regiment was ordered to participate, but never got overseas before the Armistice was signed; and in 1920, they were sent to the Panama Canal Zone on a mission of guarding the Gatun Locks. For the next 23 years, they remained in the Canal Zone.

In June 1943, the "Golden Dragons" were ordered back to the States to participate in World War II. They were sent to France to assist the 71st Division in the European Campaign against Germany, remaining in Germany until September 1946, when they were inactivated.

On October 1, 1948, the 14th was reactivated at Camp Carson, CO, as the main component of the 14th Regimental Combat Team assigned to the 5th Army with the mission of mountain warfare.

On August 1, 1951, the 14th Infantry personnel and equipment was assigned to the 25th Infantry Division then fighting in Korea. The 14th then moved to Korea, where it replaced the 24th Infantry Regiment, which was being inactivated as part of the integration of the army.

According to the thorough history of the 14th and through their performance in the various wars, the Golden Dragons were proven to be well deserving of the slogan "The Right of the Line."

• • •

25th Infantry Division - "Tropic Lightning"

The 25th Infantry Division was created from elements of the famous old Hawaiian Division at Schofield Barracks, Hawaii, on October 1, 1941. Following the attack on Pearl Harbor by the Japanese on the morning of December 7, 1941, and the machine-gunning of its own installations, the Division moved to positions on the beaches anticipatory to the defense of Honolulu while imminent danger of an invasion continued.

The shoulder patch of the 25th was adopted in September 1944, and is in the form of a taro leaf in red with a yellow border, and a bolt of lightning superimposed in gold. The taro leaf is reminiscent of the Hawaiian birthplace of the 25th.

*The 25th Infantry Division
(Tropic Lightning)
shoulder patch…*

*The 14th Infantry
Regiment
(The Golden Dragons)
Emblem*

M4A3 E8 Sherman Medium Tank

The taro plant has arrow-shaped leaves and is native to the Pacific Isles. The root-stock of the leaf is a food, the flesh of which is similar to the potato. It is used in preparation of poi.

After serving in WWII throughout the Southwest Pacific against the Imperial Japanese aggression and after the Guadalcanal campaign, the division's nickname "Tropic Lightning Division" was adopted. Although the nickname had been carried by the division, unofficially, since December 1942, it was recognized as the official special designation of the division in July 1953.

On July 5, 1950, the "Tropic Lightning Division" was ordered into combat to Korea. On June 25, 1950, the North Koreans crossed the 38th Parallel and invaded South Korea, which was the beginning of the Korean Conflict that President Harry Truman first referred to as nothing but a "police action." Police action or war, the Tropic Lightning was now called to action.

On August 1, 1951, the Department of the Army released the 24th Infantry Regiment from assignment to the 25th Infantry Division and officially assigned the 14th Infantry Regiment to replace it. In late August, the 14th Infantry arrived from Japan. The personnel of the 24th were then incrementally assigned to other units of the 25th Division, including the 14th Infantry. By September 15, 1951, the 14th was declared combat ready and then the 24th was officially inactivated as the 14th replaced them on the line.

◆ ◆ ◆

At this time during the Korean War, the armed forces became racially integrated. Some of the white soldiers had some misgivings about having black soldiers working with them, but they soon found out that they were no different than whites. That is, most were good, but a few maybe not so good. They even found out that most blacks were great guys and damn good soldiers. Personally, I found them to be alright. I had no trouble with them. I had two blacks in my tank while in Korea, plus I had one Native American, all at separate times. I found them all to be pretty good guys and good soldiers. They were men that I would have been willing to serve with in any situation.

We didn't see much prejudice in our outfit. Except, one time while in reserve, there was a young married GI that was of the LDS faith (Mormon) that wore what the Mormons called "garments" as underwear. Some of the troops teased him about wearing them, but most of it was all in fun. However, when his wife sent him an air mattress to use with his sleeping bag, a few of the guys who didn't like his religion were a little jealous. One evening, while he was out of the tent, these same guys snuck in his tent and cut up his mattress.

A Chaplain prepares to lead religious services for Soldiers of the 24th Infantry Regiment (Deuce Four) on a hillside in Korea in early 1951. The 24th was the last all-black infantry regiment in the US Army after President Truman ordered the military integrated. Two Soldiers of the 24th were awarded the Medal of Honor for heroic service "above and beyond" in the Korean War.

I guess it caused a lot of fuss within the company, but I never heard what was done about it. My platoon was on the front lines at the time, so we only heard about it, but by the time we got back to reserve, everything appeared to be pretty much the same, so I guess it was all smoothed over and everyone ended up being friendly again. Anyway, nobody bothered the young GI again. Other than that particular incident, I never heard of anyone showing any prejudice or being biased toward anyone, not on religion, race, or anything else.

Major General Ira P. Swift was the commander of the 25th Division at this time. He had been commander from July 14, 1951 to July 18, 1952. He was our commander during my entire hitch in Korea. One of the tank commanders in our outfit named their tank after him, "Swift's Premium."

By this time, we had reached our destination and had completed setting up our reserve area. The next morning after chow, we were called out again to receive our orders of what platoon, tank, and crew we would be assigned to. I was assigned to Tank 26 of the 2nd Platoon as the driver, but that later changed. Others assigned to the tank were 2nd Lieutenant Samuel Huey Epps, platoon leader and tank commander; SSgt. James (Jimmy) Talarico, gunner; PFC Bob Baxter, assistant driver (bow gunner); and PFC Melvin Simmons, loader. Lt. Epps was an army reserve officer after serving in WWII. He was from Mobile, AL. Talarico was a draftee from Boston, MA. Baxter and Simmons were draftees, both from Georgia.

Talarico had been one of the transferees from the 89th Tank Battalion, of the 25th Infantry Division. He had been a driver while in the 89th and had been in Korea for about three months before he transferred to the Tank Company. I guess he was pretty upset about being assigned as a gunner, so he came and asked me if I would please consider trading him positions. He said that he hadn't had any experience in gunnery and had no idea how to shoot one of those big cannons. He seemed to be pretty worried about it, so I told him that we should go talk to the lieutenant. So, with the permission of our platoon sergeant, MSgt. James, we went to meet with the lieutenant.

While there we explained Talarico's problem. Jimmy told Epps that all he had done was drive and that he didn't know anything about the big gun. I didn't really want to trade positions with him, but he appeared pretty worried about it, so I told the lieutenant that I had had a lot of gunnery and I didn't object if it was alright with him. After some consideration, Lt. Epps said it was fine, if we both agreed. So, we made the change and I became the tank gunner. Jimmy was a great guy; he appeared to be very grateful and relieved. I was looking forward to driving, but after a while I got over it and Jimmy and I became great buddies and very close.

101

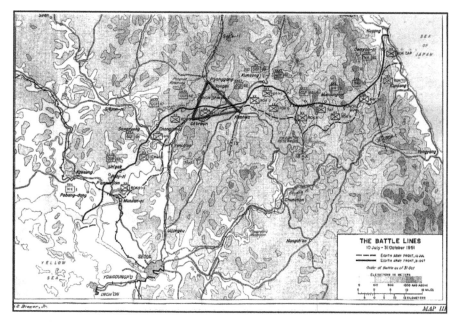

The above map shows the battle line (solid line) at the time we set up on the front within the Iron Triangle (outlined in red)...

*Photos of North
Korea just north
of the front lines
near Kumwha in
the Iron Triangle
- Oct. 1951*

Talarico (Jimmy) was a little Italian kid from Boston. We nicknamed him Boston Blackie after the detective in the Boston Blackie movies that actor Chester Morris played in. So, we just called him "Blackie" most of the time.

Blackie had been transferred from the 89th Tank Battalion, also attached to the 25th Infantry Division, to the Tank Company of the 14th Infantry Regiment. When he found out that I was from Wyoming, he told me that he was with a guy from Wyoming in the 89th. I asked him if he knew his name and he said, "Yeah, it's Mathson." I said, "Jack?" and he asked, "Do you know him?" I told him, "Yeah, I know him; hell, he's one of my best friends, and he's also from Evanston, WY."

Blackie then told me that they weren't very far from where we were and that he could take me there if we could get permission to go. We both went to see our platoon sergeant, MSgt. James, and asked him if we could have the rest of the afternoon off to go see a guy in the 89th. We explained why and what it was all about. Sgt. James was older than the rest of us, probably in his late twenties or early thirties. He was from Texas and he was regular army. He had served in WWII. He was a pretty good guy and had no problem with Blackie and me going to the 89th.

With Sgt. James' permission, Blackie took me over to where the 89th Tank Battalion's was. He apparently knew that his old company and platoon would be there, because he took me right to Mathson's tank. They were all busy cleaning and servicing the tank and equipment and didn't notice when we walked up to them. Jack had his back turned and didn't see us until I tapped him on the shoulder. He turned around and when he saw me, he couldn't believe it. He called my name, but didn't know what else to say, and grabbed me and gave me a big hug.

After introducing me to his crew, we sat down and visited for a while. It was great seeing him and quite a surprise being 8,000 miles from home and running into each other like that and having a chance to visit. He left the states for Korea about a month earlier than I had, and I'm sure he had already been in combat, but he never said much about it.

When Blackie and I returned to our reserve area, we spent the rest of the afternoon working on our assigned tank and getting it ready for combat, because in the next day our platoon was scheduled to go on front line duty. Our tank number was 26, the lead tank of our platoon. Other tanks in the platoon were numbered 22, 23, 24, and 25. Lt. Epps, our platoon leader and tank commander, named our tank in honor of his wife with the name of "Alabama Gal." Nobody objected to the name. We all just figured he was the boss.

After getting our tanks and equipment prepared, early the next morning the 2nd Platoon pulled out of the reserve area heading to the front to set up in a blocking position on the front line. We positioned ourselves along the front with about 80 to 100 yards between tanks located about 300 or 400 yards to the southwest of Hill 1062, one of the highest hills in the area. The hill was saturated with the enemy, North Koreans, which we called "gooks." Our Tank 26 was located on the west end from the rest of the platoon near the river.

The front line was specified as the MLR (Main Line of Resistance). It was approximately 155 miles across, which was from one coast of Korea to the other. It extended from the Sea of Japan on the east coast to the Yellow Sea on the west coast. The front, lying east from the junction of the Imjin and Hantan Rivers was known as the Wyoming Line and to the west was the Kansas Line. Apparently, we were positioned on the Wyoming Line, kind of ironic being from Wyoming.

In arriving at the front, we noticed that the country was mostly hills. We were sitting in a valley surrounded by hills with small mountains in front of us and behind us. A river was nearby where we could get water, when necessary. Hill 1062 was so close that you could see enemy trenches and bunkers in some areas with the naked eye. Being new to the area, we had no idea what to expect. We knew we had to do something, and fast. We didn't want to take the chance of not being prepared for whatever might happen, and being on the front, you could expect most anything. So, we got busy working on our location, first clearing a spot for the tank. Getting the tank in position, we then started on our bunker.

Each tank crew had to build a bunker and dig a trench about 12" wide, 24" long, and 18" deep for a latrine near their locations. We all spent the rest of that day building our bunker, using nothing but tank tools— ball-peen and sledge hammers, picks, shovels, chisels, etc. We had no carpenter tools or nails. We used wooden ammo boxes from our tank ammo, tarps, sand bags, and dirt (sand, if we could find any). Thank God it was still nice weather in September.

We first dug a hole about 8 or 10 foot square and about 3 feet deep. We used the shovel and pick from the tank, plus our small trench shovels to do the digging. We had to go by the river or somewhere close to fill 200 or 300 sand bags and carry them to the tank. After digging the hole, we stacked sand bags on each side about three feet high, leaving an opening for a door. The roof was made of boards from ammo crates covered with a tarp. We had no saws and we had no nails, so we used our trench knives, chisels, and ball-peen hammer to cut the wood, and wire to splice the boards together for length. Then we used a few poles for inside to brace and support the roof we covered with sand bags. We had to leave a small 3 to 4-inch hole in the roof for a smoke stack. We had to stack plenty of sandbags on the roof to make sure it wouldn't leak and for additional protection.

Our first bunker that we built located on the front lines near Kumwha in the Iron Triangle - Oct. 1951

Lt. Samuel Epps giving crew members haircuts on position of the front lines - Oct. 1951

SSgt Dennis Ottley standing in his underwear and barefooted, PFC Melvin Simmons putting used ammo casings together for the stove pipe, and Cpl. Bob Baxter looking on... (1951)

After building the bunker, we used more ammo boards to build our bunks for sleeping (5 bunks), plus we used empty 76 mm brass and empty .50-caliber ammo boxes to make a stove for heat. We used the .50-caliber ammo boxes for the base of the stove and 76 mm empty casings for the stove pipe. We applied mud and tape around the smoke stack hole to keep it from leaking. Building the bunker was quite a process. We had a little trouble fixing the roof so it didn't leak, but after using more tape, tarps, and mud packs, we got the job done. We must have got the job done right, because it never leaked while we were there.

It was a full day's work, building the bunker. After the long day, we were all pretty tired and ready for a good night's sleep. Our tank was all serviced and ready to go, ready for action. It was loaded to its capacity with ammo and fueled up. We were prepared and ready in the event we had to make a fast move.

The mess truck would come up from reserve once or twice a day to deliver chow to the troops. We took our mess gear and canteen cups to the truck to fill up with food and drink. I never drank coffee while I was in the army; I never could acquire a taste for it. So, when I went to the truck to get my chow, I always filled up my cup with black coffee and gave it to those in my crew to share, because most of them drank coffee. We were always glad to see the mess truck, because the food was pretty good, considering.

My wife, Sandy, would send packages with food quite often, mostly dry foods such as Lipton's chicken noodle soup. Mixed with hot water, it was delicious and all the crew shared it. When someone in the tank got food from home, they would always share it with the rest.

Sandy also sent me pocket books (paperbacks) to read. I wasn't much of a reader prior to going into the service, but in Korea, I did a lot of reading. I read mostly western stories and some mystery stories by authors like Mickey Spillane and others. Sometimes, while you were waiting for more orders to come out, you had plenty time to read.

When someone went back to reserve for additional supplies, they would sometimes grab a large can of cheese and some crackers from the mess tent, that is, when the mess sergeant wasn't looking. I guess it was actually stealing, but we thought it was alright and did it anyway. We called it confiscating. We also got cans of sardines quite often from somewhere and ate them with our crackers. They were pretty tasty. Sometimes, we would even confiscate cans of peaches or pears. They were real tasty.

We also kept a large supply of C-rations in our bunker and in our tank. While we were in blocking position on the front lines, the mess truck brought our chow every day, but sometimes we would eat some of the C-rations between trips to the mess truck. Actually, I didn't mind the C-rations once in a while. They were a hell of a lot tastier than what we all envisioned them to be. However, I would have hated to have had to live on them, they really weren't that good.

Some days when we were actually out in combat all day long on a raid or an assault on a hill or something, the C-rations were basically the only thing we had to eat. We always kept a pretty good supply of them in our tank. They helped us keep going.

C-rations came in a box and you didn't know what you were getting until you opened the box. Everything in the box was in cans, even the crackers. When you opened a box, you might get beans and wieners, spaghetti with meatballs, ham and lima beans, slices of ham, jams of different flavors that all tasted the same and crackers, but you didn't know for sure until you opened the box. So, if you didn't like something, you might try to trade with someone else. There was a lot of trading by crew members. The meatballs were probably the worst tasting of all. The crackers with jam weren't so bad; most of the guys liked them pretty well.

Trying to open one of the little cans was probably the worst part of the C-rations; especially with one of those little GI can openers they called a P-38. They were called P-38 because they figured it took that many stabs to open one. If you were very hungry, you needed to start early trying to open a can, or you could be either damn hungry or even lose your appetite by the time you got one opened. The good thing about the rations was that you could eat them hot or cold, it really didn't matter much, they still tasted the same.

Periodically, we got what they called cigarette rations that included cigarettes, a beer or two, and candy bars. The candy bars were known brand bars such as Hershey, Snickers, Baby Ruth, and others. Those that didn't smoke, would trade their cigarettes to those that smoked for their candy, and the same with beer. Most of the GIs smoked, but there were some that didn't drink or smoke, so there was some trading done.

All of our food that wasn't in cans was kept in metal containers because of the rats. We never seemed to have much trouble with them, but hearing some of the horror stories told about the GIs that did have trouble, it made us be even more aware of taking good care of our food, because that is what attracted them. We also kept the poison pills scattered around our bunker, inside and out.

While on the front, we had to sleep with our clothes on, so we kept ourselves and our clothes as clean as possible. If we didn't, we would get pretty stinky. To wash up and stay pretty clean, we would take what the troops called a "whore's bath" most of the time, using our helmet as a wash basin, but sometimes we did get to go down to the river and brush up a little more, never getting completely undressed. At times, it could be a little awkward.

To wash our dirty clothes, we would sometimes go to the river and scrub them on rocks, and sometimes we would also boil them, but once in a while, we would wash them in gasoline and diesel mixed. When we used the fuels to wash them, it made our clothes stink so bad it was pretty uncomfortable sleeping in them, so we didn't do that very often. How we washed our clothes and bathed ourselves depended a lot on the weather and the situation we were in at the time.

We also had to take turns standing guard duty every night while on the front lines. Each crew member had to take their turn, including the tank commander, no matter what their rank was. We each took a turn for an hour at a time. We would stand up in the tank in the commander's hatch with the M2 carbine and our pistol, plus we always had the top machine gun loaded and ready for action. We never knew when we might be attacked, so we had to really pay attention to what was going on around us. We were only a few hundred yards from the enemy.

Standing guard at night could get pretty spooky. Standing up in that turret, and watching out around the area while trying to stay awake, and not daring to fall asleep, could get damn scary. If you stared at one thing long enough, like a bush or some object, it could look like it might be moving and tempt you to shoot, so you didn't want to stare at an object very long. You had to look away from it for a second and then look at it again to make sure you were seeing things right.

Yeah, guard duty on the front lines could get real spooky, especially at night. A guy did a lot of thinking while on guard duty, but he had to stay wide awake and very alert, and expect just about anything.

Up on the hills behind and above us, were quad-50 crews dug in, and quite often they would fire at the enemy across the valley over our heads. Quad-50s were four .50-caliber machine guns attached that they used for long-range firing. They would fire these guns two or three times a week, sometimes in the daytime, but at night, you could see the tracers flying above your head, so we knew when they were firing.

Quad-50s were set up with ammunition that had a tracer shell every 5th round. A tracer shell was a bullet that would light up. When they fired at night, it would look like a steady lit up line of fire flying overhead. They were firing at different enemy targets across the valley. It was pretty neat watching that line of fire going over our heads and it did help keep you awake while on guard duty. It also seemed to make the time go by faster just watching them, but it did worry us a bit. We were afraid if one of those quads fell it could cause someone to possibly be seriously hurt, but nothing ever happened, at least as far as we ever heard.

Solon Tells House Members How Yank Fighters Assist Kids

WASHINGTON—"I think the entire world should be interested in a great humanitarian project that is being conducted by American fighting men in Korea," said Rep. Foster Furcolo (D., Mass.) at a recent meeting of the House of Representatives in Washington.

Furcolo said, "I have just been informed of it by Cpl. Lionel Barrow, Springfield, Mass., who is a member of our Armed Forces fighting in Korea.

"IN A LETTER to me, he tells the story of a combat unit's drive to help 108 North Korean orphans through the winter. Let me emphasize that the orphans being aided are North Korean orphans.

"The units involved are the 25th Tropic Lightning Division's tankers—the 89 Medium Tank Battalion (commanded by Lt. Col. William Hamilton), and its attached organizations, Company A, 79th Medium Tank Battalion and the 14th Infantry Regiment Tank Company."

FURCOLO THEN READ Barrow's letter to the House. "To the Chinese Communists, Task Force Hamilton means blazing 76s and certain death, but to 108 children between the ages of two and 15 in an orphanage in Seoul, it means candy and security against the hard winter which will soon be on us.

"It may seem incongruous to some people that a battalion of hard hitting tankers, who spend their days and nights killing and being killed, should also be willing to prevent death by providing the money which will feed, clothe and shelter 108 North Korean orphans they have never seen. But it doesn't seem so to us.

"WITHIN THE WEEK the 89th Tank Battalion of the 25th Division will have turned half of a needed $1650 over to the UN civil assistance command for the He-Myuhg orphanage in Seoul.

"The money will be used by the UNCAC's public welfare officer, P. G. Cross, to buy shoes, woolens, fuel, supplement their diet, put windows in the somewhat wrecked building.

"AS ONE CONSTANT visitor to the orphanage explained, 'not high-heel shoes, silk panties, nylons, lip-stick, semiformal party dresses. Necessities, not frivolities.'

"However, this is but one part of a two fold plan. There is a definite need for aid from organizations in the states,' Cross said. 'Units like yours (meaning the 25th Division) can come to the rescue in an emergency such as exists today, but it takes an outfit permanently located like a church or a well established social organization to provide the steady flow of goods and money that is needed.'

"PART TWO of the plan calls for getting a personal contact between the tankers and the kids, having the tankers write to their families, friends, etc., and interest them in sending the needed items overseas on a regular basis."

At that time, tanks didn't have heaters or air conditioners, so it could get damn hot or damn cold in the tanks; it just depended on how hot or cold the day was. During the summer months, the temperature would get well over 100 degrees, and in the winter, the temperature would get way below zero at times, especially at night. The climate in Korea had a lot of humidity and could get damn cold in the winter.

Therefore, you could roast in the summer or freeze to death in the winter if you didn't wear enough clothing. That's why a lot of troops called tanks "hot boxes" sometimes, and "ice boxes" other times, depending on what time of the year it was. They also called them "iron coffins," you can imagine why.

The only way we could get warm in the winter was to stand over the engine grill on the back deck, but you couldn't do that while in battle. When we stood guard duty at night in the winter, it could get damn cold. During that time, we always wore two or three layers of clothing to help keep us warm, plus, we always tried to stay as dry as possible.

It wasn't very long after we had set up our reserve area and got well organized, our unit, the Tank Company of the 14th Infantry Regiment, agreed to unite with other tank units attached to the 25th Infantry Division in a drive to help approximately 108 North Korean orphans between the ages of two and fifteen. The orphanage would be located in Seoul and would give them food, clothing, and shelter through the hard cold winter that would soon be upon us. The units of the 25th that were involved in the project were the 89th Tank Battalion, Company A of the78th Tank Battalion, and our tank company.

CHAPTER 12

FIRST COMBAT MISSION

Although the talks for an armistice had been going on since July 10, 1951 at Kaesong, there was no progress made and the truce talks came to a stalemate. Then on October 25, 1951, the talks were moved to Panmunjom and negotiations reconvened, causing the Korean War to become a seesaw situation. However, the Iron Triangle appeared to be a very important location for the United States and the United Nations to continue to hold onto at all costs, and so the conflict continued.

About October 4, 1951, our platoon leader, Lt. Epps, had gone back to reserve to a meeting, apparently concerning an attack on a hill. When he returned, he informed us that on October 6, 1951, the 2nd Platoon would take part in an assault on Hill 404. The order was that we would temporarily leave our blocking position and participate in supporting an infantry patrol from Company I of the 14th Infantry Regiment in attacking Hill 404. The assault came off with rather spectacular success. It was reported that 18 of the enemy were killed, 2 were wounded, and heavy damage was done to the enemy's position.

During this assault, I was in Tank 26 with Lt. Epps as commander and myself as gunner. This would be my first experience actually firing the 76 mm cannon in combat. During that day, we fired an awful lot of 76 mm ammo at different targets, while giving the infantry support as they advanced up the hill on foot. I had never fired that gun so much in my life.

It was quite a day. I believe that we all got a lot of experience during the assault, plus, I kind of got to like the position of being a gunner. From all reports, we had done a tremendous amount of damage to the enemy. The infantry was also very successful in their attack with very few casualties.

During the attack, we were advancing slowly behind the ground troops with open hatches. The entire crew had their hatches wide open, except me. The gunner doesn't particularly have a hatch; he just sits down in the turret below the commander looking out his telescope. So, the only thing he can see is what the telescope allows and the targets that he shoots at. Unless there is close contact with the enemy infantry or artillery, tankers prefer to keep the hatches open. It was much easier to watch around you with open hatches.

Although we were somewhat worried about the tank killer teams (bazooka squads) that we were previously told about, and the possibility of any enemy ground troops that might sneak upon us, we did keep our machine guns loaded and ready to be used, if needed. We always had our equipment in good shape and ready to use when necessary. We were also concerned about any artillery that may be coming in on us, but on this day, there were no problems...thank God.

• • •

Before I left home, while on furlough, Sandy had bought me a Zippo cigarette lighter, the only type of lighter that worked well in the wind, and there was plenty of that in Korea coming off the Yellow Sea and the Sea of Japan. She had my name, plus the city and state engraved on the lighter. I smoked at the time, and I had that lighter with me all the time while in Korea. A lot of the troops, whether they smoked or not, carried Zippo lighters.

Also, the little black book of the New Testament that I picked up in Chicago, while on my Christmas furlough, was also something that I carried with me all the time while in Korea. I carried that little book in the left breast pocket of my fatigues. I always considered myself a Christian and felt like I had nothing to lose by having that book with me all the time while in combat. When it came right down to it, I guess I did put a lot of trust in God that I would get home safely. I know I did a lot of praying during the time I was in Korea.

• • •

After our first experience of real combat, we returned to our blocking position on the front lines. All five tanks returned to the same location that they previously had. Thank God for not having to build another bunker; the ones we had built previously were still in place. This helped make our day, not having to build again. We were kind of worried that we would be setting up in different locations and would have to build new ones.

114

The next day after returning to our positions, we heard that Lt. Epps may have volunteered our platoon to take part in the assault on Hill 404. This kind of upset some of the men. One crew member was really pissed off, as we found out later. Some thought that by him volunteering our platoon, it made him look like he was going to be what we called a "gung ho" officer. I personally had a lot of respect for him.

We were kind of pissed off also because after we had taken Hill 404, a few days after our troops pulled off, it was once again occupied by the enemy. I guess that's why they called it a seesaw war. Sometimes we took territory and then gave it right back to them. I suppose that our leaders were just interested in holding the present position. It seemed a little ridiculous to most of the troops, running a war this way, but those in power made the decisions and maybe they were right... who knows.

•   •   •

On July 10, 1951, the beginning of the peace talks, the war entered a new stage and at this time, the battle line was fairly stabilized. It seemed that the 25th Division engaged mostly in tank-infantry patrolling, raids, and aggressive assaults to maintain contact with the enemy, to detect any forward movement of enemy positions, and to capture prisoners; but, their biggest interest was holding their position in the Chorwon-Kumhwa area, the Iron Triangle.

After General MacArthur was relieved as supreme commander of the Far East, General Matthew Ridgeway was named to replace him. Ridgeway and the departments in Washington, DC, all felt that there were sound reasons for not maintaining the UN advance as far as the Yalu River. As Ridgeway put it, "It would not have been worth the cost. It would have widened our battlefront from 110 miles to 420. We stopped on what, I believe, to be the strongest line on our immediate front." Putting the war in what some called a "condition of stalemate."

Most of the troops didn't appreciate the way the war was going. They would have rather been fighting a war to win and then go home, but the situation was at a standstill and there didn't seem to be any interest in advancing with the idea of gaining ground or winning the war; we were just to hold our positions for the present. The way things were going wasn't doing any good for the morale of the troops, but for the time being, they were accepting it.

Keeping up morale is difficult in any combat situation, but when the fighting devolves into a prolonged stalemate such as the war was in at this time, it was particularly hard to maintain. Both sides continued to exchange artillery fire, conduct raids and patrols, and occasionally attempted to seize a mountain peak here or there, but for the most part, the battle lines remained relatively the same.

The worst part was that we all knew that Russia and China were supplying and equipping the North Koreans with weapons, men, and all kinds of supplies. This made them a little pissed off that President Truman stopped us from doing the job we knew we could do, if only given the chance. Some thought that doing so could have saved a lot of lives and probably would have helped Korea become one nation.

However, it didn't happen that way so the troops just obeyed the orders from the top and accepted what was happening. They just hoped that the President and his commanders knew what they were doing. After all, they were in charge and maybe they were doing the right thing. Who knows?

•   •   •

When we returned to our position from the battle on Hill 404, we dug in again and continued to work on our tank and equipment. We had to swab out the 76 mm gun and clean the breach, getting it ready for the next time. After every use, we had to do this to keep our weapons in good shape. Keeping your equipment and weapons in good condition and ready to go was always essential and very necessary. When the ammunition truck arrived, we restored our tank with a full load of ammo. The tank held 70 rounds of 76 mm.

Most of the 76 mm ammo we carried in the tank was HE (high explosive), but we had to have 10 or 12 rounds of AP (armor piercing) and a few rounds of WP (white phosphorous) ammunition, because we never knew when we might need that type. The AP ammo was normally used against enemy tanks, armored vehicles, and sometimes fortified bunkers. WP ammo was usually used as a blind or to force the enemy out of a well-secured area. The rest of the ammo was HE, which we used 99.9 % of the time. All of the 76 mm ammo had delaying fuses in case we ever needed it. At any rate, we had to be prepared for any situation and for the next mission, which would only be a few days away. Our tank now was ready to go and so were we.

Sure enough, Lt. Epps volunteered his platoon again, so we heard, to go on the next attack on a hill. Twice in a row it had been said that he had volunteered the 2nd Platoon into battle. So far, no other platoon in our company had seen any actual combat. I never knew why, I just figured that it was because we were already up at the front and were always ready to go, but some of the men thought it was because Lt. Epps was just another "gung ho" type of guy and wanted to make himself look good by volunteering us. In a few days, we would be leaving our position, once again, to assist another infantry unit(s)

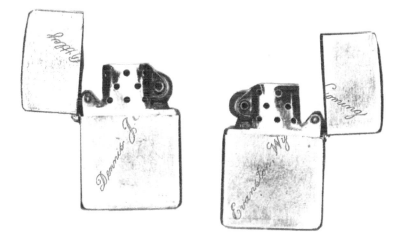

The "Little Black New Testament" book that I carried with me in my left breast pocket all the time I was in Korea in 1951-1952.

The "Zippo" cigarette lighter that my wife, Sandy, bought me before I left for Korea. It was about the only lighter at that time that would light in the wind, and at times Korea was windy.

Photo taken from Tank 22 while giving support to the infantry on another numbered hill...

Tanks giving heavy fire support to the infantry while attacking a numbered hill...

PFC Chester Renfrow, loader on Tank 23 standing next to the M.L.R. sign
(Main Line of Resistance)... These signs were placed all along the front...

The M.4A3 E8 "Sherman" medium tank was sometimes called the "Easy Eight."
It was considered to have a powerful and reliable liquid-cooled V-8
Ford gasoline engine with a capacity of 168 gallons of fuel.

The 50 cal. machine gun
was normally used on top
of the turret for aircraft attacks
and well-fortified bunkers,
but we sometimes interchanged
it for the 30 cal.

Each M.4 Sherman tank
normally had two 30 cal. machine
guns, one in front of the assistant
driver and one in the turret
in front of the gunner.
Sometimes we put one on top
of the turrent in place of the 50 cal.

The M1911 is a single-action, semi-automatic, magazine-fed, recoil-operated handgun chambered for the .45 ACP cartridge...

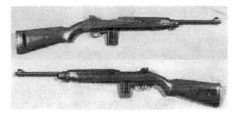

The M3 submachine gun, 45-caliber, sometimes referred to as the "Grease Gun"...

The M1 and the M2 are both lightweight, easy to use carbines. We had the M2 in our tank, which is full automatic...

The Mk 2 grenade is a fragmentation hand grenade highly used during the Korean War...

from the 14th in raiding another barren hill. All the hills in the area seemed to be badly damaged from all the artillery fire, air fire, automatic weapons, anti-personnel mines, etc. There were no signs of wildlife or any vegetation, just barren hills.

All the time I was in Korea, I never saw any wildlife, except the rats. In the valleys, there were bushes and groves still remaining, but the hills all seemed so bare. It's kind of a shame because I believe, under normal circum-stances, the country would have been quite beautiful. It would have had nice colorful scenery with the hills, mountains, valleys, and rivers throughout both North and South Korea, but the war ruined that.

There were also a lot of damaged and destroyed tanks and other vehicles still lying around on the roadsides and in the valleys, damaged by the war. Some of them looked like they had been blown up and burned. Some were friendly units and some were the enemies'. We heard a lot of very unpleasant stories about what had happened. Seeing all this and hearing the stories caused a guy to do a lot of thinking on just why in the hell are we here in a country that we had never even heard of prior to coming, but I guess there was a good reason. We, at least, stopped the aggressive communistic movement through-out the world by being there, so they said.

It's been said: "The soldiers fight, and the kings are the heroes."

CHAPTER 13

A DAY NEVER TO FORGET

A few days after we returned from our first mission, Lt. Epps was, once again, called to discuss another mission for our platoon. When he returned, he informed us that we were chosen to participate in another raid on another hill. I don't remember the number, but I do remember it was an 800 something number. I remember the hill was supposed to be heavily fortified, and from what the lieutenant said, it was very important that our troops take it over. It was another hill in the area of the Iron Triangle .

Therefore, on October 10, 1951, we headed out, once again, on a mission to support a raid on another hill, again, volunteered by Lt. Epps; only this time, we would not be so lucky. Twice now our platoon had been called out to take part on an assault, supporting an infantry unit from the 14th while the other platoons remained in blocking positions on the front line, just because Epps volunteered us a second time.

As we pulled into position to fire at the enemy while supporting the ground troops with heavy fire power, I was in the gunner's seat, so I didn't see much of what was going on, but apparently, as we found out later, the loader of Tank 22 had pulled his .45 automatic and had it aimed at Lt. Epps with the intent of killing him for volunteering us. As far as I know, his tank commander, SFC Blair, stopped him. We didn't know about this until we all got back to reserve, at which time SFC Blair reported him. The GI was then disciplined and transferred out.

As far as I know, Lt. Epps never volunteered our platoon again, but we were being continuously called out to participate in battles on the various hills in the area while we were located on the front line, but so were the other platoons. It seemed like we were all pulled off the line to assist some infantry unit in raiding a hill about once or twice a week.

While located in our present position, for the next four or five months we would also be called on to support infantry units from the 35th and the 27th Infantry Regiments, plus, later in the winter, we would be called to assist units of the Turkish and the Greek armies.

Anyway, during the day of the raid on the 800 numbered hill, we continued to fire on the hill, and I was really having a ball with the big gun, firing at the enemy bunkers, trenches, and machine gun nests. During the shooting, Lt. Epps noticed a gook sticking his head up over the ridge like he was observing our position. The lieutenant asked me if I could see him and, looking through my telescope, I said, "Yes, I see him. He's been sticking his head over the ridge off and on for the last few minutes as if he is making fun of us and daring us to try to get him." Lt. Epps then said, "Can you get him?" I said, "I can sure try. Do you want me to?" Epps replied, "You're damn right; blow that son-of-a-bitch to hell!" So, I zeroed in on the ridge about 300 yards or so away and fired my first round, hitting just below the ridge. I thought that would scare him a little, but once again he stuck his head up over the ridge like he was still daring us to get him.

So the lieutenant, really pissed off by now said, "Can you get him this time?" I said, "Let me try something different." I wanted to try another approach because I was afraid if I tried to hit him directly, I would just either hit the ridgeline or go over him. Epps said, "Yeah, go ahead, but get the bastard." So, I told the loader, Simmons, to put the next round on delay action and load it, so he did. He reached over and gave me the usual pat on the shoulder, indicating that the gun was loaded and ready. I then, using my telescope, zeroed in for the edge of the ridge, and making sure of my shot I called out, "On the way!" and in a split second, I fired.

•   •   •

While in training on the big tank guns, 76 and 90 mm, we were trained that as soon as the loader throws a shell in the breach and it's ready to fire, the loader is to pat the gunner on the shoulder or knee or somewhere, indicating that the gun is loaded and ready to fire. The gunner then checks his sights and makes sure he's on target. He then calls out, just before he fires, "On the way," giving warning to the rest of the crew, who would probably be looking out of the hatch to watch where the shell lands. Calling out would give them a chance to shield their eyes from the muzzle blast.

•   •   •

It was a great shot. The shell hit right on the ridge of the hill, ricocheting off the ridge into the air and exploding just above where the gook was sticking his head up. It was a dandy of a shot, the best I would ever make. It was a surprise to everyone, including me. We never saw the bastard again. We either got him or scared the hell out of him. At any rate, he never stuck his head up again, at least not while we were still there on that day. Epps was so surprised, he shook his head and said to me, "Ottley, you have got to be the best damn gunner in Korea. I don't think any other gunner could have made that shot." All I said was, "I guess it was just a lucky shot and God was with us," but it was good. Our loader, Simmons, said, "Way to go," and I thanked him for putting the shell on delaying action. At any rate, I was pretty proud of it, but I probably couldn't have made a shot like that again in a thousand years.

We then continued opening fire on the hill, giving support to the troops as they advanced up the hill toward the enemy. I'm still down in the gunner position, not knowing exactly what was going on, when the lieutenant called us to hold fire. I had no idea why, but apparently, some major and his driver from the 14th Regiment drove up to talk to the lieutenant. He told Epps that he had seen that shot at the gook sticking his head up and was amazed, but I was down in the gunner seat where I couldn't tell for sure what they were talking about, only what I heard later.

I don't recall the major's name, but apparently he had asked Epps to have our tank follow his jeep up this certain road around to the right of the hill and advance closer to the enemy, for some reason or other. I never heard why, but the lieutenant did as the major requested. So, Epps pulled us out of our position and we started following the jeep, leaving the rest of the platoon behind to support the troops as they advanced.

It seemed like we had gone about a half mile or so when we came to a stop. Epps got out of the tank to talk to the major. Apparently, the major and his driver had spotted an anti-tank mine just a few feet ahead of us. They talked for a few moments and decided that they better not go any further. Apparently, at the time, they decided to call the demolition squad to come and dig the mine up, because in about a half hour the squad showed up. The rest of the crew got out of the tank to see what was going on. I was the only one left in the tank, and I was getting pretty damn tired of sitting down in the gunner's seat, not knowing what was going on. So, I decided to get up out of my seat and see what it was all about. I stood up on the commander's seat where I could see the crew working.

Watching them from the tank, I could see that they were being very careful about how they dug around the mine, trying to get it out of the ground. It took them a while, but they finally got it out without any problems. From where I was, the mine looked like it was nothing but a wooden box about 6 to 8 inches deep, 12 to 15 inches long, and 8 to 10 inches wide. I found out a little later that the box was wooden, filled with explosive powder, and had a delayed action type fuse.

After the demolition crew left, taking the mine with them, Lt. Epps told everyone that we best back up and get the hell out of there, because there were probably more mines ahead of us, and the major agreed. So, I got back in my gunner's seat, and Epps got back in the commander's spot, while the rest of the crew got back in their positions. Epps then instructed Talarico to back the tank up slowly. I don't believe we went back any more than 50 feet, when all a sudden, I felt a hell of a strong jolt and the tank rocked like it was about to turn over…thank God it didn't. It felt like we were in an earthquake.

What happened was when they backed us up, we drove over the same mine that we had already driven over, apparently tripping the delayed fuse. When we hit it the second time, it blew our left track. It blew the track completely off. When I got out to see what happened, about half of the track was setting on top of the tank, the other half was lying on the ground. It just barely missed hitting the lieutenant and Simmons. They were both standing up out of the turret. I believe it scared the hell out of all of us; I know it did me.

We came to find out that the mine we hit also had a delayed action fuse. That's why it didn't go off the first time we drove over it. They told us later that the North Koreans set their anti-tank mines up with the delayed fuses so that when a number of tanks went up a road that was mined, the first tank wouldn't cause it to blow, but maybe the second tank or the third tank would. The tank(s) following might not be driving in the same track or, for some other reason, it might miss the mine all together, but chances were one of the tanks following would blow it, causing all the tanks in the lead to be trapped with nowhere to go except back. Being blocked in like that could make it tough on the lead tank(s) when trying to get around the damaged tank, depending on the terrain, but at any rate, the lead tank(s) and damaged tank would be in a very dangerous and deadly situation. Fortunately, we were the only tank in our platoon on the road, as the rest were still supporting the infantry with fire power while attacking the hill.

The entire crew got out of the tank onto the ground, looking the situation over…all except me. I did get out of the gunner's seat and moved over to the loader's compartment. Standing up on the loader's seat about waist high out of the hatch, I could see the damage pretty well. It looked like about half of the track was laying on the ground and the other half was laying up on top of the engine grill behind the turret.

The lieutenant called up to me and asked me if the radio was working. After a few minutes trying to get the radio going, I had trouble getting any reception from anyone. Our platoon's radio code was "BUFFALO," but I just couldn't seem to get any reception whatsoever from anywhere. I kept trying, time after time, to call and repeating, "This is Buffalo 22, come in," trying to reach one of our other tanks, but no answer. Apparently, the mine had also blown our radio. So, I told Epps that the radio was completely out. At that time, he approached the major, who was still with us, about calling headquarters to get a tank retriever out there to pull us back. The major did, with no hesitation.

It seemed like it took forever, waiting for the retriever, but they were actually there in about an hour or so. As soon as they got there, they proceeded to hook the tank up. Just before the retriever crew had arrived, everyone except myself was on the ground, looking over the situation. I was still up in the loader's hatch, trying to do something with the radio, plus I wanted to make sure the machine gun was loaded and ready, in case of a ground attack.

We had the .30-caliber mounted on top of the turret at this time. The .50-caliber machine gun is the standard weapon on top of a tank turret, but there hadn't been any air attacks from the enemy in the area for quite some time, thanks to our air force who had done a great job keeping them back, so we thought it best we have the .30-caliber mounted in it's place. There was more of a chance of having a ground attack than an air attack under the present circumstances.

While waiting for the retriever to show up, Lt. Epps told Blackie Talarico to get up in the turret and help me, and be alert in case of any trouble. I guess we all had a funny feeling sitting there like a duck in a shooting gallery, feeling very vulnerable. When Talarico got up in the commander's hatch, we both proceeded in trying to get the radio operating, but we never could.

So, in trying to get ready for any possible trouble from the ground, we made sure the .30-caliber machine gun was loaded and ready, hoping and praying that we wouldn't have to use it. I reached down in the loader's hatch and grabbed the M2 carbine and the M3 submachine gun (grease gun), making sure they were loaded and setting them on the turret in case we needed them. Meantime, while sitting there, waiting for the retriever crew to get us hooked up, all hell broke loose.

Heavy artillery started coming in from the North, causing everyone on the ground to scatter just as the retriever almost had us completely hooked up. I don't know why the gooks didn't start throwing artillery at us sooner, but I was damn glad they hadn't.

When we started getting shelled, the retriever crew, the major and his driver, and Epps, Simmons, and Baxter all headed for cover. Talarico and I were up in the turret, but before we could get down in the tank and button up, the second round of artillery hit just to my left rear about 10 steps away, wounding Talarico. A large piece of shrapnel had hit him in the left side of his body, just above his hip. He yelled out to me that he had been hit, so I immediately pulled him down inside the tank on the loader's side and laid him out on the tank floor. About this time, Epps came out of cover with Simmons and, not knowing, yet, that Talarico had been wounded, told Simmons to get up there in the driver's seat, and hold the right lever back as he was going to try to get in the retiever and pull us back out of range. I don't know what happened to Baxter, our assistant driver, but I know Epps didn't want to wait around for him, so he told Simmons, who was close by, to get in the driver's seat.

Artillery fire was coming in pretty heavily, so the major and his driver got in the jeep and scrambled out of there, finding cover. The retriever crew all scattered running, trying to find cover, and trying to get out of range. I wasn't sure where Baxter was, but I'm sure he was also trying to get the hell out of there and out of range.

I was down in the loader's compartment with Talarico strung out on the floor, practically scared out of his mind, which I believe we all were—a crippled tank, a wounded comrade, and nowhere to go—what could you expect? I unbuckled his pants belt, undid his pants, and pulled up his shirt to take a good look at the wound. He seemed to be bleeding pretty badly, so I asked Blackie, "Where is your pistol belt?" and he replied, "Down under the driver's seat." Well, I wasn't about to take time out to look for it and Simmons was too damn busy trying to hold that right lever back while the lieutenant was trying to pull us out of there. So, knowing I shouldn't, I grabbed my own first aid packet off my belt to use on Blackie. I thought to myself *he's just losing too damn much blood*, so I immediately proceeded to set the packet on the wound and wrap it around his waist really tight and tying it.

In the meantime, the lieutenant and Simmons were trying to pull us out of there, while three or four more rounds of artillery came in on us, not hitting the tank…thank God. Everyone else, I guess, was running back for cover. I couldn't see them, but Epps pulled our tank back very slowly because the retriever crew only had time to get us partially hooked up.

Inside the tank, I was trying to take care of Blackie. He was kind of hysterical. He was damn scared and kept asking me not to leave him. I assured him that I would not leave him under any circumstances. He said, "I want to go home, I'm scared and want to go home; I don't want to die." I said, "Blackie, just take it easy and try to keep your head. I'm damn scared, too, and so is everyone else, but just take it easy and hang in there. I'm not going anywhere without you; we will make it, we will get the hell out of this mess. Okay?"

The lieutenant got us pulled back about a quarter of a mile when the retriever came loose again. Thinking we might be out of range of the enemy artillery, I jumped out of the hatch, but I was wrong. They started blasting at us again, so I jumped back in the tank and buttoned up the hatch. Epps ran for cover in a grove of trees on our right, where I believe the rest of our bunch was; the major and his driver with the jeep, the retriever crew, and Baxter were somewhere in there, but I couldn't see them.

Proceeding to tend to Blackie for the next few minutes, him begging me not to leave him, I assured him time and time again that I would not leave him and that we would make it out of this mess. I said, "Blackie, let's just hope and pray that none of those rounds hit our tank or the retriever. The best thing we can do right now is keep praying to God that we get out of this mess."

Artillery still coming in, Simmons still in the driver's seat with his hatch buttoned up, when all of a sudden, taking a peek out of the hatch, I saw the lieutenant come running toward our tank. Under the artillery that was still coming in, he was trying to get us hooked up once again and get us the hell out of there. I jumped out of the turret, asking him if he needed any help. He said, "No," then I told him that Talarico had been wounded by shrapnel, and that he was kind of out of his head. He then said, "Get back in there and take care of him, and tell Simmons to keep that right lateral pulled back tight and for heaven's sake, button up." So I did.

More artillery coming in made it tough for Epps. He hit the ground three times while trying to get us hooked up. I wanted to get out there and try to help him, but he said he would be okay and I was worried about Blackie. So, I stayed inside the tank trying to sooth him and praying to God that one of those rounds didn't hit the tank.

Epps finally got us hooked up, then got in the retriever and pulled us out. He pulled us about two more miles, finally out of the range of enemy artillery. At that time, everyone seemed to show up. The major called for an ambulance for Talarico. When the medics got there with the ambulance, they immediately changed the dressing that I had put on him and told us that it was a good thing we dressed his wound when we did because he had already bled a lot. There was a lot of blood on his clothes, the floor, and commander's seat. We helped them get Blackie out of the tank and then he was gone before I knew it. I wanted to talk to him again before he left and was taken away because I knew he would probably be going home, and I would never see him again and I never did.

He was taken to our reserve area where one of the helicopters, nicknamed "whirlybird", "eggbeater", "airdale", whatever, picked him up and took him to a MASH (Mobile Army Medical Hospital) unit for treatment, and then to a military hospital in Japan, and then home.

All the time I was in Korea, I had never heard that the medical units were called MASH until I saw MASH on television years later. I had no idea why, but no one in Korea ever talked about a MASH unit that I had heard; they always referred to them as a medical unit, or station, or something. Maybe I just wasn't paying attention, but I was quite surprised when I saw the program on TV years later.

The retriever crew checked the cable and made sure we were hooked up alright, then they got back in their retriever and pulled our tank back to reserve. This time, Baxter showed up and was now in the driver's seat. We would be in reserve for a while, waiting for another tank, which would be there in about two days. By this time, we figured that the rest of our platoon would be back on the front line in their previous positions.

When we got to reserve and settled down a little, headquarters immediately called me for questioning about Talarico's .45 automatic pistol and his pistol belt. They hadn't found either, yet, and were concerned where it might be. They apparently didn't like losing weapons, but I told them as far as I knew, it was under the driver's seat when Talarico got wounded, that he always took it off to drive. I told them that I asked him where it was so I could use his first aid packet to dress his wound and he had told me it was under his seat. I told them that I did not want to take the time looking for it because he was bleeding so badly, so I used my own. I got a lecture for that, but apparently they did find the gun and belt where he had said it was.

When I went to supply to get my first aid packet replaced, I got another lecture from the supply sergeant. He told me at first I couldn't have one, because a GI was not supposed to use their own packet on another GI. I told him that I was very much aware of that, but I didn't think I had time to look for his, that we were getting blasted and I wasn't even thinking about what the rules were. I just wanted to stop him from bleeding and get us all the hell out of there. He finally gave me the packet and kind of apologized and said he understood.

We were in reserve for about two days when we finally got another tank. We immediately started working on it, getting it ready to go back to the front where the rest of our platoon was. We completely serviced and cleaned the tank, dropping the inspection plate, and all. We also loaded it up with a full load of ammo and made sure we had all our weapons cleaned and in working condition. Lt. Epps had the motor pool crew paint the name of "Alabama Gal II" on both sides of the front of the tank. We now were ready to return to the front.

The next morning, we returned to our position on the front line with our new used Sherman tank. Our bunker was still there with all our belongings in place. Everything appeared to be just like we left it. While back in reserve, we got a chance to shower, but we still had the same clothes on that we had on when we hit the mine, so we got busy setting up again, washing our clothes and all.

The next day, Lt. Epps was called back to reserve. He was called back because he was being honored for his fast thinking and the courage he showed getting us out of the mess we were in from hitting that mine. He was to receive

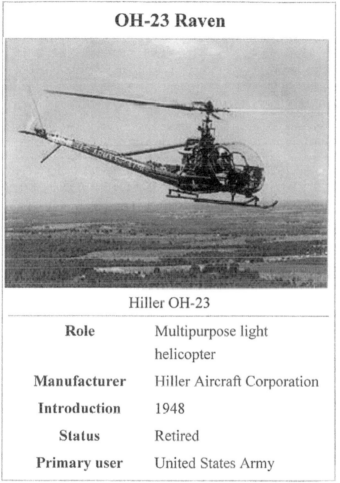

OH-23 Raven

Hiller OH-23

Role	Multipurpose light helicopter
Manufacturer	Hiller Aircraft Corporation
Introduction	1948
Status	Retired
Primary user	United States Army

The OH-23 Raven model could carry litters on the skid supports making it possible to evacuate two wounded soldiers at a time from the battlefield. It was also used for reconnaissance and command and control in the Korean War. Some called this model an egg-beater and some called it a whirlybird, but whatever you called it, it was very useful during the war and saved a lot of lives. The pilots of this aircraft put themselves in danger many times.

the "Silver Star" for valor. He also had been promoted to 1st Lieutenant. It was great that he got the honors, but some of the guys were quite surprised and wondered about it.

I thought it was great, although, I did think that it was mostly his fault that we got into the mess to start with, because he had separated us from the rest of the platoon, which was, according to the book, a no-no. However, I felt that what happened wasn't intentional and that he shouldn't be critisized too much for it.

In training back in the States, they always told us that you should never break up a platoon of tanks unless, of course, the situation called for it and it was absolutely necessary, but if you do have to, always make sure that you have at least two tanks staying together. Never let a single tank wander off alone; you need to have at least another tank with you so that you can protect each other. They also told us that you and your crew should never leave your tank for any reason, unless it is on fire, out of commission, or under fire. At any rate, I still had a lot of respect for the lieutenant and thought the promotion and the medal were well deserved. He was a good officer.

Before returning to the front, we were sent a new replacement for Talarico. He actually replaced Bob Baxter, who the lieutenant named to take Blackie's place as driver and the new replacement, PFC Art Topkin, would take Baxter's place as our assistant driver or bow gunner, whichever you wanted to call it. Topkin was from Nevada, so now we had two westerners in our tank, myself and Topkin.

During the next week, we were called out on two more raids on a couple more hills; I don't recall the numbers. We were supporting two different infantry units to overrun more hills. Both times went similar to our first time out, when we went on the raid taking Hill 404—very successful with very few casualties.

Thinking back to when we hit the mine, I got wondering why Talarico got hit and I didn't, because I was standing up out of the turret just like he was and the shell hit closer to me than it did him. So, I got to thinking maybe it was because I had my little black New Testament book with me in my left breast pocket, which I always carried while I was in Korea. I thought to myself *could that have had anything to do with it?* To this day, I have always felt that the little black book may have helped in keeping me safe from harm while there. Anyway, I have always been glad I had it with me.

• • •

"In war there are no unwounded soldiers…"—Jose Narsky

Cpl. Melvin Simmons, loader stading in front of Tank 26 (Alabama Gal II)

Crew of Tank 26 (Alabama Gal II), left to right: Lt. Samuel Epps, platoon leader and tank commander; SSgt. Bob Buxter, driver; Cpl. Melvin Simmons, loader; PFC Art Topkin, assistant driver. Photo taken by SSgt. Dennis Ottley, gunner...

Members of the 2nd Platoon, Tank Company, 14th Infantry Regiment... Left to right: Cpl. John Cole, loader; SFC Carnes, tank commander; Cpl. Sparks, assistant driver and SFC Blair, tank commander at Command Post (reserve)...

Command Post (reserve area) neasr Kumhwa and the Iron Triangle

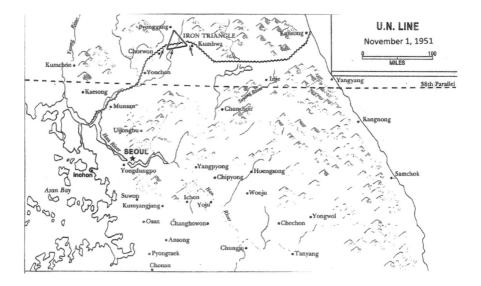

U.N. LINE
November 1, 1951

0   100
MILES

CHAPTER 14

A STAR COMES TO KOREA

I t was now November and it was getting cold. We were expecting snow anytime. We hated to see winter come, because we had heard stories of how cold and miserable it could get in Korea. Our tanks had no heaters, so we knew we would be standing guard duty up in our tanks, colder than we cared to imagine, but we tried to dress for it by wearing double sets of clothing. Sometimes, we wore as many as three pair of socks at the same time just to keep our feet warm and dry.

I remember, about this time, I had to take a crap and grabbing some paper, I went to our fancy latrine, a long hole in the ground. I pulled my pants down getting ready to do my job, but when I bent down my right knee, a trick knee they called it, flipped out and almost caused me to fall in the damn hole. I caught myself okay, but it hurt like hell and was paining pretty badly.

After finishing my job and completing the paper work and all, I pulled my clothes up, having a hell of a time because of my knee paining so badly, but I finally made it. When going back to the bunker, I had to do everything I could to keep from limping. I was afraid that if the lieutenant saw me limping, he might send me back to reserve to have my knee looked at by the medics. I didn't want that because there was a chance they might have sent me home because of a bad knee, giving me a physical discharge. Thank God it never went out again while I was in Korea. I always made an effort to be very careful, especially when I took a crap or while climbing on and off the tanks. There was no way I wanted to be sent home for that reason.

So, when I got back to the bunker, I did everything I could to keep the rest of the crew from noticing me, but I couldn't help from limping a little. Lt. Epps did notice it and asked me why I was limping. I told him that I just

137

turned my ankle a little and that it would be okay. He accepted my explanation and nothing more was said about it, thank God.

We were now doing everything we could to try to keep warm, especially at night. We had our little stove in the middle of the bunker made out of empty 76 mm ammo casings for pipe and an empty .50-caliber ammo box for the burner. We mixed gasoline and diesel for fuel. Even though our tanks burned only gasoline, we always had some diesel fuel on hand for cleaning tools and other reasons.

Lt. Epps was called to headquarters, once again. Only, this time, it was for something other than attacking a hill. It was for something quite unusual and completely surprising. When he returned, he told us that we were going to have a visiter from Hollywood, that actress/singer Monica Lewis was coming to Korea. We all said, "Who's that?" and he said she was a new actress/singer and new to Hollywood, and that she wanted to adopt the 14th Infantry Regiment because she had heard that we were new to Korea. For that reason, she made the announcement that she was adopting the 14th and would be paying the regiment a visit. Everyone seemed to think that was great and was anxious to see her, but we on the line were never to do so. The lieutenant informed us that he was ordered to pick one guy out of his platoon to be one of her chaperones, and that he wanted our imput, but nobody said anything or gave any suggestions, so after some thought, he picked SSgt. Bob Baxter, our driver. He said that being as Bob was single, tall, and not bad looking that he would be a good choice. After hearing about it, some of the guys in the platoon were kind of upset about the selection, but I really didn't give a damn. I figured that it wouldn't have made any difference even if I had, plus it wouldn't have mattered who he picked, there would have still been someone upset. I thought it was a pretty good choice.

I think the biggest reason they were upset and maybe even a little jealous about it was that Baxter would be the only one that would get to see her, because she would only be able to visit our reserve area. There was no way they would have allowed her, under any circumstances, to come up anywhere near the front lines, because it was just too dangerous. Plus, they weren't about to let any more of us go back to see her. They weren't about to leave the front unguarded.

After the event and her performance was over, Baxter returned to our bunker. He reported to us on how much fun he had and how he enjoyed her show, that she had a great voice, and that she was "beautiful," as he put it. He said there were a hell of a lot of GIs at the show and that they all seemed to really enjoy her. He told us that she got a standing ovation. He just kept on boasting about how great she was and how much he enjoyed her, and kept

Monica Lewis – 1950

Monica Lewis in Korea – 1950

rubbing it in, trying to get everyone's goat, until the lieutenant finally told him to knock it off.

Baxter was gone for just a couple of days. During that time, we had nothing else to do except keep the equipment up and take our turns at guard duty. We never left our bunker, except going to the mess truck, getting our chow, going to the river to wash some of our clothes, or going to the latrine. It was early November, so during the daytime it was still a little warm, but it got damn cold when that sun went down.

The next day, it snowed about three inches, just enough to make the ground wet, slick, and sloppy. Lt. Epps had left to go back to headquarters for orders that our platoon would be going out on another raid, supporting the infantry attacking another hill. I don't remember the hill number, but it would be within the same area, the Iron Triangle.

After hearing the news, we immediately went to work double-checking our tanks to make sure they were all ready to go. We wanted to make sure they were all fueled up and had a full load of ammo. We always kept our tanks ready, but any time we got orders to go out on an assignment, we always double-checked everything to make sure we didn't miss something or that something may have gotten changed.

The next morning, we were ready to move out. Lt. Epps' tank took the lead and I was still his gunner, but this would be the last time that I would be gunner on Tank 26, "Alabama Gal II." After this day, I would be assigned to another tank.

They declared the raid to be another big success. There was a lot of damage and casualties of the enemy. Again, there was a minimum amount of loss on our side, but the infantry did have a few wounded.

Returning to our position on the line, we immediately cleaned and serviced our tank, getting it ready for the next assignment, and continued taking our turn on night guard duty, watching the lit up tracer bullets from the quad-50s continuosly firing over our heads from the hills behind us.

• • •

Phonetic Alphabet
The following phonetic alphabet was used by the military to ensure clarity in radio/telephone communications during WWII and the Korean War. It was also used for clarity of titles such as A Company would be described as "Able" Company, B Company would be "Baker" Company, and so forth:

Able	Jig	Sugar
Baker	King	Tare
Charlie	Love	Uncle
Dog	Mike	Victor
Easy	Nan	William
Fox	Oboe	X-Ray
George	Peter	Yoke
How	Queen	Zebra
Item	Roger	

•   •   •

CHAPTER 15

A PROMOTION, ANOTHER TANK

After we got back from the raid a day or two later, Lt. Epps made the announcement that SFC Blair, Tank Commander of Tank 22, "Doris," would be going home. He stated that Blair had his 36 points plus of combat time in and was eligible for rotation, and that he, the lieutenant, would be assigning another person to replace him as tank commander of that tank.

I guess it gave us all something to think about, but I had no idea what would come next. The lieutenant took me aside and asked me how I would like to be the commander of Tank 22. I looked at him and said, "I thought you would probably pick one of his crew members for the position." He replied, "No, I don't think any of them are ready for it at this time, but I do feel that you are, and you sure as hell deserve it, but," he continued, "I hate like hell losing you as my gunner." I thanked him for that and said, "Yes, I'd be glad to accept the position and thanks for your confidence in me; I really appreciate it. Plus, the increase in pay from the promotion will be a big help to my wife."

The next morning, Lt. Epps and I went over to let the crew of Tank 22 know that I would be moving in with them as their new commander. I was damn glad the lieutenant was with me to make that annoucement, because it made it a lot easier for me. When he told them the news, looking at their faces, you could see the resentment in some of the crew. After Epps left, I did get kind of a cold reception from some of them, but I guess that was to be expected.

The crew and I already knew each other, so it wasn't like I was a stranger. So, after sitting down and talking about what they could expect of me and what I would be expecting out of them, they seemed to be more relaxed. I told them that they had a job to do and that I also had a job to do, and the best way to get the job done would be for all of us to work together. I told them that if they had any suggestions or advice to offer me, I wanted them to speak up, because I was always willing to listen. I also told them that the one thing that I would be very fussy about was keeping our tank, our guns, ammo, and all other equipment in good condition and always ready to go. I then added that if we did all this, we would all get along fine and things would work out really well.

The next thing I did was get the driver, SSgt. Harry Grey, to assist me on looking the tank over. While inspecting the tank, I wasn't sure just how to tell Harry, but I was not satisfied with the way the engine looked. So, I just said, "Harry, how long has it been since you guys dropped the inspection plate on this engine?" The inspection plate is directly under the engine and should be dropped when cleaning and servicing. He kind of looked at me like he wanted to say something like, "What's it to you?" but he just said they had never dropped the plate since the the tank was assigned to their crew, and that Sgt. Blair didn't think they should drop the plate while on the front lines. He made a good point, but then I said, "Harry, we've dropped ours twice on Tank 26 since we've been up here." He may have been a little pissed, but he agreed with me to drop the plate and give the tank a good service job and clean it up. Then I told him that I would go over and ask Lt. Epps what he thought about dropping the plate. I said, "I'll be right back," and left.

I left and went over to Tank 26 and told the lieutenant what happened. I asked him if he thought it would be alright if we dropped the inspection plate while we were on the front. He said, "Sure, go ahead, it's pretty quiet up here right now, but," he continued, "get it done today. I don't want to see you having to work on it after dark." I said, "No problem, we'll be finished way before dark, and we'll be cleaning all of the weapons, as well."

So, when I returned, I told the crew what Epps said, that we had his permission to drop the plate, but we had to have everything put back together before dark, and I assured him that we would. "We will also be cleaning the guns while we are at it," I added.

So, the rest of the day, we put all of our time on the tank and the weapons. At first, I was afraid that the crew would be down on me, but I was wrong; they all pitched in. I never heard anyone bitching. Matter of fact, they appeared to be in great spirits like they were glad to be doing something. As far as I was concerned, I thought to myself, *they are going to make a great team.*" Sgt. Grey was a good driver, and after a while, Sgt. Blades got to be a good gunner.

At this time, my crew consisted of SSgt. Harry Grey, driver; SSgt. Jim Blades, gunner; PFC Ted Davis, assistant driver or sometimes called bow-gunner; and PFC John Cole, loader—a great bunch of guys. Jim Blades was from New York City, but I don't recall where the rest were from. But, after a while, things started working out pretty damn well and I was really looking forward to having a great crew. At this time, everyone appeared to be happy and satisfied.

However, the next morning when Lt. Epps came over to our tank to see how we were doing, he said he saw some gooks on his way over here walking up a trench on Hill 1062. He said he could see them with his naked eye and wanted us to fire on them.

So, at that time, he told Blades and Cole to get in the tank and get ready to fire on them. He said if we didn't hit them, at least we'd scare the hell out of them. So, Blades and Cole got in the tank with the lieutenant acting as commander, and he gave them the order to prepare to fire. Cole loaded the gun, patted Blades on the leg, indicating that the gun was loaded and ready. Epps gave Blades the estimated distant (in most cases, the commander gave his estimated distance to start with, and it was up to the gunner to figure the rest out after his first shot). So, Blades set his sights, called, "On the way," and fired. The shell hit way short, but the first shell is not expected to hit the target. So, Epps ordered them to fire again. This time, the shot was still short.

Then Epps, acting a little disappointed, told Blades to hit the target this time or at least get close enough to scare the hell out of them. Cole loaded the gun, Blades prepared to fire, taking careful aim, and called the signal. Blades' shot was way over this time. The lieutenant acted really pissed off; he called out and said, "Ottley, get up here and show this guy how to fire this damn gun!" This was something I was hoping wouldn't happen.

So, I climbed up there, feeling like hell and damned embarrassed. I could imagine how Blades felt, but I did what the lieutenant wanted, waiting for Blades to get out of the gunner's seat. Then Epps said to me pretty damn loud, "Get down in the seat and show them how to hit a target." That made me feel like crap and damn embarrassed for Blades. I could just imagine how he felt, but I went ahead and climbed down into the gunner's position like the lieutenant requested.

As I climbed down into the tank, I hoped to hell that I would be lucky enough to hit the target and do what Epps expected of me. So, Epps called the order to prepare to fire, Cole loaded the gun, patted me on the leg, and I was ready to fire, waiting for Epps to give me his estimated distant. The distance he called out was a little different than what he gave Blades to start with, because after three shots he had a little better idea of what the distance would be. This gave me a little advantage over Blades.

Blades stood behind the turret, watching where the first shell hit. My first shot was just a little short, so Epps called out to fire again. So, Cole loaded the gun again, patted me on the leg, I took careful aim, called, "On the way," and fired. The lieutenant called out, "Great shot," and said, once again, "Ottley, you have got to be the best damn gunner in Korea!" Then he added, "I think I will demote you back as my gunner on Tank 26." I was hoping that he was only kidding, and he was.

I really felt bad about Blades; he had heard what Epps said and acted quite resentful as he climbed off the tank, not saying anything. I wanted to talk to him really bad, but I thought it would be best to wait a while and let him do a little thinking about what happened first.

After Epps got through looking the tank over, he seemed to be well satisfied with what he saw, then left, and said, "Keep up the good work; it looks like you're doing alright." I knew that Blades' feelings toward me wouldn't be good and I knew he would be more resentful than ever. Blades might have been resentful and pissed off and not saying a word to anyone, but he did tell Cole to give him a hand and, at that time, they immediately started cleaning the big gun again because it had been fired. The only one he talked to for a while was Cole, his loader.

Finally, Blades came to talk to me. He asked me what he was doing wrong, and I told him that it is hard for me to explain to him just what he was doing because I wasn't paying any attention when he was firing for the lieutenant. I just told him that when he's in the gunner's seat, to be relaxed and take everything into consideration, including the movement of the tank every time he fired, because the blast of the gun sometimes causes the tank to move a little—not much, but enough to cause your shot to be off some. He said to me, "Yeah, that makes sense. I had never been told that, but it makes a lot of sense." Then I said, "And, take your time when adjusting your sights after each shot; don't rush yourself, the target will more than likely still be there."

He thanked me for the advice and left. I hoped he left thinking about what I had told him. I guess he did because he became a damn good gunner, plus he and I got to be great friends. He ended up being my gunner the entire time I was in Korea. The entire crew, with the exception of John Cole, my loader, was with me throughout the time I was in Korea. We had three more loaders after him.

We finally got the orders that we would be going on another raid the next day, supporting a unit of one of the companies of the 14th Infantry Regiment. This would be my first time on a raid as tank commander.

So, now we had our orders that our platoon was to be ready to roll first thing in the morning, ready to move out. We were heading for another hill, supporting another infantry unit with heavy fire power, and that we should plan on being there all day.

This being my first experience on a raid while tank commander, I had a much better position to see what was going on around me than I had when I was gunner, stuck down in the gunner's seat and not being able to see much of anything that was going on. That was probably the worst part of being a gunner, but now I was able to sit up out of my seat at least shoulder high and sometimes even higher.

As we advanced toward the hill, I was able to see the infantry in action as they advanced. I was amazed at how brave those foot soldiers appeared to be, rushing up the hill, most with their M1 rifles and BARs, some with heavy machine guns and mortar equipment, throwing hand grenades when necessary, and dodging enemy fire. This was the first time I had seen them in action and, again, I was amazed—they were under fire, trying to dodge not only rifle fire from the gooks, but also machine gun fire, mortar and small artillery fire, and trying their damnest to watch out for anti-personnel mines. I saw them constantly falling, mostly to keep from getting hit, but sometimes not getting up. I said to myself, "Those boys are real heroes; they have no protection to speak of, but they just keep moving forward, never retreating. Yeah," I again said to myself as I watched them, "those troops on foot have got to be the real heroes, and I'm damn glad I'm a tanker." However, there is still a lot of danger in being in the tanks, but at least you have got some protection.

Tankers can also be very vulnerable, at times. There were tanks completely demolished still lying around throughout Korea that you could see just about anywhere. These tanks had been hit and destroyed by artillery fire, some by napalm bombs and gun fire from enemy airplanes that had been furnished by the Russians, plus anti-tank mines, and bazooka teams. In most cases, some crew members were killed and wounded and, in some cases, the entire crew was either burned alive or shot to death, not being able to get out of their tank. War was hell and damn dangerous, no matter what outfit you were with.

It was just another long day. The infantry won another battle, another hill, the attack was over and our platoon was ordered to return to our position on the front. It was a good day for us. I learned a lot just being in the position where I could see what was going on, and Sgt. Blades seemed to improve every time he fired the big gun. He got to be just as good on the gun as any gunner in Korea, and maybe even better than most.

We had now returned to our position and our bunker on the front. We were all worn out and ready to turn in, but we still had to worry about someone taking first watch of guard duty. PFC Ted Davis volunteered to go on guard first, and said he would wake someone up in an hour to relieve him. Ted was a great guy and a real sport.

The first thing the next morning, Blades and Cole immediately started cleaning the big gun and we restored the ammo when the truck arrived. Grey and Davis cleaned and fueled the tank, ready for another trip.

SSgt. Jim Blades, gunner, on left and Cpl. Ted Davis, assistant driver, on the right cleaning and servicing some of our weapons on Tank 22 while on fronr lines...

SSgt. Jim Blades, gunner, on left and SSgt. Harry Grey, driver, on right cleaning and servicing Tank 22 on the front lines. Note: the inspection plate dropped

SFC Dennis Ottley, Tank Commander of Tank 22 walking back from meeting with Lt. Samuel Epps, Platoon Leader on next assignment...

.. SSgt. Harry Grey, driver of Tank 22over-looking the area while on the front lines...

One of our tanks of the fourth platoon that was damaged by an anti-tank mine is being pulled back out of range of enemy artillery by another tank and a retriever which we called a mule train when it took more than on vehicle to pull a damaged tank out.

A 25th Infantry Division foot soldier firing a BAR (Browning Automatic Rifle) while advancing on a hill in North Korea

The suffering of the Korean civilian refugees who fled before the advancing Chinese armies was made much worse by the terrible winter weather. Here in January 1951 a refugee column moves south along Korea's eastern coast.

CHAPTER 16

LT. EPPS' ACCIDENT, A NEW LEADER

A day or two went by when we got the word that Lt. Epps was going to be gone for a few days. He and a couple other lieutenants from the tank company were scheduled to go to some kind of seminar or meeting for officer's in Chin-Chon, Korea. They went there in a jeep that they had checked out at the motor pool. Apparently, they never took a designated driver, they drove it themselves.

On their return trip, they had a bad accident. We heard that they had been drinking and having a pretty good time when they ran off a bridge and turned their jeep upside down in a creek bed. We never did hear who was driving, but all of them were hurt pretty badly. Luckily, someone came along not too far behind them and spotted the jeep.

They never made it back to the company. We never heard how the others were, but Lt. Epps was hurt so badly that they had to send him to a military hospital in Tokyo. It was four or five weeks before he returned back to our platoon. In the meantime, our platoon would be assigned a new platoon leader.

Our new platoon leader was a new young officer that had just recently finished OCS (Officer's Candidate School). If I remember right, he was from Virginia. He was a second lieutenant named Maguire. I don't recall his first name, but he was assigned to Tank 26 to replace Lt. Epps until he returned, but we were under the impression that because of his injuries, he might just go home, rather than back to the front.

Our platoon was still in position on the front line. When the new lieutenant arrived, his first duty, apparently, was to visit each tank in his platoon and get acquainted. He appeared to be an alright guy and, in time, the entire platoon got to like and appreciate him.

His biggest problem was that he had never had any combat experience and he wasn't too proud to admit it. He never hesitated a bit to ask for help and advice, mainly from his tank commanders. However, he found out real fast that Sgt. James, our platoon sergeant, wasn't the one to get much advice or help from.

Sgt. James was a likable guy, and he had been in the army for quite some time, but he didn't seem to have much army savvy, especially in combat. He seemed to know quite a bit about his duties as a state-side garrison soldier, but he wasn't too swift on reading or understanding military maps or tactics. Some of the troops wondered just how in the hell he even got to be a master sergeant, but he was and no one questioned it, but he was teased a little by some of the troops.

I remember one time after we tansferred to Mundung-ni Valley in the spring of 1952, we came underfire. This particular day, we drew fire from the enemy when Sgt. James jumped under his tank and said they were shooting at him because they saw his stripes and knew he was one of the leaders. He took quite a razzing from his crew over that incident.

Before every assignment, the tank commanders would meet with the platoon leader to go over the map and the plan of attack for the next raid or attack—when and where we would be going, who we would be supporting, and what was expected of our platoon. I'm not sure why, but Sgt. James often came to me for help on reading the maps and getting advice on the various assignments. I helped him a lot, just like I would help anyone that needed it, but some of the other tank commanders got a little pissed off when I helped him. They thought that he should go to the lieutenant to get the help. That way, the lieutenant would find out just how much the sergeant really knew about military maps and tactics. Maybe they were right, but I couldn't deny him the help. I got into a fist fight with SFC Carnes, commander of Tank 24, over it. The fight didn't really last long; they broke it up before either of us got many licks in. I told Carnes that I was going to help anyone that needed help, whether he liked it or not. We shook hands and were good friends after that. Carnes was a good commander and he had a good crew.

Getting back to Lt. Maguire, who needed all the help he could get because he was so young and inexperienced… During the short period he was with us, we were assigned to go on quite a few more raids. Some of the outfits we supported while he was our leader, besides infantry units from the 14th, were brigades from the Turkish and the Greek armies, plus a few infantry units from other regiments of the 25th Division.

One day, Sgt. Blades and I got talking and I said to Blades, "I've heard that Lt. Maguire's dad is a congressman in Washington, DC." Blades said to me, "You don't say dad, you say father." When he said, that I thought I was talking to a school teacher. It really took me by surprise because I hadn't realized how uppity Blades was until then, but other than that, he always seemed like an alright guy and we did get to be good friends. Blades was from a well-educated family in New York City and was raised to be pretty formal, but I was just a down-to-earth type of guy from the West and hadn't had that kind of upbringing.

Anyway, when Lt. Maguire came to visit our tank, I asked him in front of the crew, "Lieutenant, we've heard that your father is a congressman in Washington, DC, is that right?" He replied back and said, "Yes, my dad is a representative out of Virginia." I could see the surprise on Blades' face when he said "dad," but nothing was said. Apparently, the lieutenant was more down-to-earth than Blades thought.

It was now mid-November with about 18 inches of snow on the ground and colder than hell; once again, we were called out on another raid on another hill. Only this time, the infantry wore white covers over their parkas so they would blend in with the snow better.

Again, I couldn't help but feel sorry for those foot soldiers. I really had to admire them and, once again, I thought to myself *yeah, they have got to be the real heroes of this war*. Watching them tramp through that snow, half of them falling, most getting up again, some not getting up at all, laying in the snow, waiting for a medic to get to them. The medics had to be admired, too, because they were in there right with them. Real heroes they were.

You just can't help but admire guys on the ground, carrying those heavy weapons, dodging all that machine gun fire, mortar rounds, and trying to watch out for anti-personnel mines, plus the artillery that was coming in. Yeah, once again, I was damn glad to be in the tanks, even though we didn't have heaters, and they were damn cold, but at least we didn't have to tromp through that deep snow like those guys did.

Like I said before, we had supported troops from Greece and from Turkey while under Lt. Maguire's command. They both were great fighters and, from what I'd heard, they loved to fight hand to hand against their enemies and weren't a damn bit scared.

Both the Turks and the Greek appeared to like the tankers a lot. They liked the heavy fire support the tankers gave. A couple of us tank commanders got acquainted with a few of the Turks when we were supporting them on an attack. After we had returned to our position on the line, a few of them visited us. They always had one or two that could speak English, so we were able to communicate with them.

When they came over to visit, they brought a few articles with them like cameras, watches, hand guns, and whiskey. We found out really fast what good horse traders they were because they sold the whiskey, which was either Canadian Club or Seagram 7, for $21 a bottle and some of the guys bought what they were selling. We found out later that when a GI went on R & R (rest and relaxation) he could buy a whole case for $21, and some did and brought it back with them. So, whoever paid $21 for a bottle of the booze kind of got stung. At that time, no one from our outfit had gone on R & R, yet, so we weren't aware of the price. Some of the guys just wanted to get some whiskey.

Some of us bought other items, mostly cameras. I bought a shoulder holster from them for a few dollars. I thought that maybe a shoulder holster would make it easier to carry my .45 than having it hang on my belt, but after about a week, I found out different. The shoulder holster wasn't all that great. Having my .45 hanging in that holster under my left arm pit wasn't very comfortable, so I gave the damn thing away. It was just too cumbersome, so I went back to my good old army issued side holster. It felt a lot better.

While in Korea, all we had was script money. Most of the guys didn't look at it as real money, so they would buy things they really didn't need just to be buying something. A lot of them gambled with it, playing poker or blackjack when they could. In some cases, that was why the Turks had such an easy time selling their stuff. Most of us bought something from them mostly just to be friendly.

While the Turks were visiting with us, they invited some of us to go over to their camp and have some of their Turkish coffee. We were told that their coffee was pretty strong. We told them we would be over if our platoon leader would allow it.

A couple of days later, some of us decided that we would go visit them for a few minutes. So, a few of us commanders went to the lieutenant and asked him if it would be alright if we made the visit. We told him that they were just over the hill a few hundred feet where we were. After a little thought, he said, "Okay, but make sure you leave at least two men on a tank behind. You can't leave a tank unattended."

Sgt. Blades and I went from our tank. There must have been six or seven of us go from the platoon. When we got there, it was just getting dark and what we saw, we couldn't believe. They were dancing around and acting up, making a lot of noise, having fun. They had a great big bonfire going that lit up the entire area. I said to Blades, "Don't they know that the gooks are just across the valley?" Blades said, "I don't know, but I don't like it and I don't want to stay very long."

When we got there, they greeted us like we were long lost buddies. We asked them if they were concerned about the enemy seeing their fire and that they might start firing at them or attacking them. They indicated that they weren't one bit worried, in fact, one of them said, "Let the bastards start something; we'll take care of them," but it did bother some of us.

So, we all sat around getting acquainted and drinking their coffee. I didn't drink coffee at that time, but I thought I would try some and it was strong, but I finally got a cup down. At that time, if I drank coffee, I used cream and sugar, but they didn't use any and didn't have any. They just drank it black.

Apparently, they really liked the tankers. They couldn't stop commenting on how much they appreciated the support that we gave them during the raids. They all seemed to be great guys and treated us really well. They, at least, didn't try to sell us anything this time. We only stayed for a short time, because it was pretty dark and I think most of us wanted to get the hell out of there before something happened. So, we thanked them for everything and went back to our own tanks on the line.

I think we all enjoyed their hospitality. It was a learning experience for us and I think most of us were glad that we went. That was the only foreign unit that we ever had the opportunity to visit while in Korea.

Just a day or two before Thanksgiving of 1951, we had been on another raid, supporting a unit from the 14th Infantry Regiment. The raid had, once again, been considered a success by the top brass, but, once again, we pulled back off the hill and, consequently, the gooks were back on the hill the next day and had control. It seemed like this happened pretty often. I guess the top commanders knew what they were doing, but it sure didn't help the morale of the troops much.

We considered our participation a success as tankers, supporting and defending the infantry as they advanced toward the enemy. Once again, we came through with no damage or casualties and, once again, I reached in my left breast pocket and took my little black book out and thanked God for bringing us back safely.

We returned to our position on the front and, again, performed our usual duties— cleaning and servicing the tank and the big gun, checking everything over, getting it ready for the next mission.

Thanksgiving was the next day. I couldn't believe that I was actually spending this great holiday in Korea, 8,000 miles from home All the crew seemed a little down, I guess because of the holiday. I got a few letters out that I had received from my wife and read them, one wishing me a Happy Thanksgiving.

That afternoon we got a big surprise, and I mean a wonderful surprise. The mess truck showed up and brought our chow; something we weren't expecting, but it sure was welcome. To our surprise, they brought us one of the best turkey dinners that I had ever had up to that time. Amazingly, it was delicious, but then maybe the reason it tasted so good was because we had been eating a lot of C-rations lately; but it was good, damn good. The first chance we got, we sent word back to reserve to tell the mess sergeant thanks a lot and how good it was.

I was hoping I would get mail that day, but, apparently, the mail jeep took a day off, although I had just received a package from my wife, Sandy, a few days before. Sandy and my mom often sent me packages. There was always something good to eat, and sometimes winter underwear and socks would be in them. I always shared the food with my crew. They loved the Lipton's soup, the hot chocolate mixes, and other foods, and they always looked forward to me getting a package.

It took about three to four weeks to get mail to and from home. Sandy wrote me a letter almost everyday, but I didn't necessarily get a letter every day. Some days, I might get as many as three letters at once because of the way the mail came in, but it was sure nice to hear from Sandy, my mom, and some-times my sister.

I took quite a few pictures with the camera that Sandy had bought me when I went in the army. Taking pictures in Korea, there was no way to get them developed, so I would send my roll of used film home to Sandy to get them developed. She would send them back to me and then I would write on the back, explaining what and who the photos were of and what they were about, and then send them back to her. She then kept them for me for when I got home. This process could take as long as two months to complete.

Thanksgiving 1951 had come and gone in Korea, and we were now back to our normal duties. Lt. Maguire was still our platoon leader.

CHAPTER 17

THE GREAT TRAIN WRECK — 1951

On November 12, 1951, there was a serious and fatal train wreck in Wyoming, just a few miles west of Evanston, my hometown. The streamliner called "City of Los Angeles," bound for Chicago, IL, was slowing down to safely pass a freight train that had just pulled into the siding, waiting for the passenger trains to go by. This was all during a severe blinding snowstorm that was caused by a high west wind.

Apparently, the block signals were working okay, but the storm was so blinding, it caused the engine crew of the passenger train called "City of San Francisco" to be unable to see the signals, or the flares left out by the brakeman of the first streamliner. Unfortunately, because of the first train slowing up, the second streamliner caught up and rear ended the first train, killing 20 passengers and crew members, plus injuring many more.

The impact was so great, it caused railroad cars from both passenger trains to fly all over the area in different directions. Some fell into the freight train parked on the siding, causing damage to it. One reporter said it looked like a war tragedy with all the cars smashed up and on top of one another. The Union Pacfic said it was one of the worst train wrecks in the company's history.

In one sharp second, Evanston, WY, a town of 3,800 residents, was wakened out of it's thoughts of the cold and miserable winter as the "City of San Francisco" rammed into the "City of Los Angeles" about three or four miles west of town. In just a matter of minutes, Evanston became a boomtown. In one jarring second from this jarring crash, Evanston jumped from a sleepy Wyoming community to the front pages of the nation's leading newspapers, including the *Pacific Stars and Stripes*.

The above photo is of the "City of Los Angeles", streamliner of the Union Pacific Rail-road. This was the front train in the train wreck that got rear ended by the U.P. R.R.'s streamliner, "City of San Francisco" on November 12, 1951 (Courtesy of the Uinta County Museum)

Photo of the great train wreck near Evanston, Wyoming on November 12, 1951. (Courtesy of the Uinta County Museum)

Photos of people from Evanston working on the train wreck
that occurred on November 12, 1951.
(Courtesy of the Uinta County Museum)

But, they said Evanston was ready. In less than an hour, the entire town from the police department, the fire department, the hospital, the two mortuaries, the Civil Defense Organization, and many more entities were functioning in high gear, helping to rescue the several hundred frightened, confussed, and hysterical passengers from the two trains.

The Uinta County Civil Defense director recruited all available doctors from a wide area. All ambulances in the region were shuttling back and forth from the crash scene to the Evanston Memorial Hospital and the Wyoming State Hospital. People with their own cars were helping uninjured passengers to town to find places to stay. The entire town of Evanston went all out, trying to help all the passengers, injured and uninjured, to be as comfortable as possible. At that time, they said that the catastrophe was one of the most tragic train wrecks in Western history. Evanston rose to the occasion in a big way.

Sandy had sent me a letter telling me about it, but I had already read it in the *Pacific Stars and Stripes*. The *Stars and Stripes* was a newspaper that was made available to all military personnel in Hawaii and the Far East. It was published in Honolulu and it's the only paper received by the troops in Korea, unless they received a paper from home. If I remember right, it was a weekly newspaper, but I may be wrong. However, I did get a letter from Sandy about three weeks later, telling me about the train wreck. I wrote back and told her that I had already read about it in the *Stars and Stripes*, but in her letter, she went on to tell me all about how it happened. She said they had been having a lot of snow with high winds, causing some very severe blizzards and sub-zero temperatures. She said that some of the blizzards were so bad that you couldn't see two feet in front of you. The schools had been shut down and the city, county, and state were all having a hard time keeping up with the snow removal.

She indicated in her letter that the train wreck was caused by the storm. Apparently, the heavy snow and wind had partially covered the railroad block signals, making it very difficult for the engine crew to see what was ahead of them. The train in the lead apparently was behind schedule, because of the weather, causing the other train to catch up.

Sandy described the tragedy as a real mess and that they had to use the schools and the churches, among other buildings in Evanston, plus the Wyoming State Hospital to take care of all the passengers on the trains. She said her dad, among many others from Evanston, went to the train wreck to help in getting the people out and transporting them into Evanston and helping to find them a place to stay. They also went out days later to help clean up the mess. Her folks were heavily involved.

Winter in Evanston, Wyoming - November 1951
Lots of snow and blinding Blizzards...

Sandy Ottley,
wife of SFC
Dennis Ottley,
with son, Randy

Randy, son of Dennis and Sandy, with puppy sitting on top of car...

Ruthie Fotheringham, baby sister to Sandy, sitting on top of car...

CHAPTER 18

PEACE TALKS GO SOUR, LT. EPPS RETURNS

We were now into December 1951 and, apparently, the peace talks taking place at Panmunjom weren't going too well. From what we had heard, there seemed to be a lot of discussion among our leaders on whether the United Nations troops should make their advance to the Yalu River or stand firm at our present location. South Korean President Syngman Rhee wanted the UN troops to invade North Korea and push the enemy all the way back to the Yalu River (the Manchurian border), but General Matthew Ridgeway, Commander of the Far East, only wanted to hold our present position, feeling that we would lose too many troops. He also wanted to keep the peace talks going, but at this time, that was a problem. I had heard that General James Van Fleet, Commander of the 8th Army, which the 25th Infantry Division had been attached to, agreed with Ridgeway. Apparently, North Korean leaders and Mao Tse-tung, the Chinese Chairman, were upset at this kind of talk, causing things to not look too good.

It looked like Syngman Rhee got his way, maybe, because at this time all troops and equipment were called back from the front to the command posts. Upon the order, we cleaned up our area and pulled our tank out of our position, only leaving our bunkers that we had built.

When we got back, we were told to make sure that our tanks were full of fuel and our ammunition was 100% fully loaded. They told us that we would be lining up to move out. We would be heading north, nonstop, except for fuel and food. Destination would be the Yalu River.

This made a lot of troops stop and think. Most of them wondered if this was really happening, or was it just another move that would never take place. However, this was something that most of the men were hoping for, "Let's get this war won and over with so we can all can go home."

163

I asked Lt. Maguire, "What and how are we going to overtake and handle Hill 1062?" He said, "Well, I think that there is only one thing we can do with it and that is just go around it."

They said the infantry would be riding on the tanks with us, at least until we got across the front lines. So, we all lined up our tanks in formation out on the road just outside of our command post, ready to pull out with the tanks pointing toward the north and all loaded up with the infantry. Someone hollered out, "Yalu River, here we come," plus there were a lot of similar remarks while we were waiting for the order to move out. Some of the troops were excited, some were scared, but most were just wondering what's next. I wasn't too excited, I was a little scared, but most of all, I was just wondering like the rest, but I was glad to see it happening. This had to be a big invasion, possibly the biggest during the Korean War; if it came off, a lot of GIs would be killed and wounded.

But, it never happened. Just when everyone was in position, waiting for the big order to move out, we got the order, completely different from what we were expecting. It was all called off. Apparently, the peace talks were back on and we were ordered to stop all activity and return our tanks to the motor pool and go back to our squad tents and relax. Most of us got a pretty good night's sleep.

The next morning, we were ordered back to our position on the front. We returned to the same location as we had when we left, our bunker still there and in the same shape as it was when we left. We put our tank in position, checked it out, and proceeded to go on about business, as usual.

One day while we were sitting around doing nothing, I noticed some commotion up on Hill 1062, so I grabbed the set of binoculars and took a look. Our air force was strafing the top of 1062. While watching them, I noticed they were Navy Corsairs, but all of a sudden, one of them got hit. Seeing the pilot bail out, I got to thinking that he would be in a hell of a position, because there was a big chance that he would probably be captured, and from what we had heard over the grapevine, the gooks were none too easy on pilots.

However, a few minutes after he had bailed out, we saw a helicopter heading toward the hill, apparently hoping to grab him before the enemy did. Later on, we did hear that the helicopter got there first and the pilot was safe. Thank God for helicopters.

A couple weeks later, Lt. Sam Epps, our former platoon leader, had returned from Japan. Apparently, he had come through the accident in good shape. I, for one, was really glad to see him back, but at the same time, I hated to see Lt. Maguire leave. I thought a lot of both of them and was hoping that Maguire would at least stay with the tank company, but he didn't; he was transferred out to another outfit. I don't recall what outfit he went to, but I felt really bad about him leaving. Hell, I never even got to see him before he left, and that made me feel even worse.

However, I was glad to see Epps back and told him so. He was a good leader and he knew what he was doing. Some of the men didn't particularly care to have him back, but there wasn't much said about it by anyone. The men had gotten to really appreciate Lt. Maguire and loved talking to him; he was a great guy.

Lt. Epps appeared to be the same person he was when he got hurt, but after our tank platoon was called out on a couple more raids, the lieutenant didn't appear to be as 'gung ho' as he was before his jeep accident. Maybe him getting hurt as badly as he did from the accident may have mellowed him out, but he still ran a good unit and he handled the raids like he knew what he was doing.

It was now the middle of December and Christmas was approaching. We would be going out on a few more raids, supporting the infantry on numerous hills between now and Christmas. During these raids, we found that there would be propaganda leaflets and small sacks of candy scattered all over the hillside. Being in the tanks, it was impossible for us to pick any of them up, but some of the ground troops that got to know us a little would pick them up and give them to us. They would climb up on the tank just long enough to hand them to me to pass them on to my crew.

We weren't sure just how they got there, but we thought they were probably dropped by air during the night. The North Koreans were great at passing out propaganda leaflets and information, trying to talk the GIs into either going home or surrendering over to their side. Thank God that very few did, but surprisingly, there were some. One of the leaflets that was dropped was folded up really tight and tied to a small bag filled with four or five pieces of candy; candy corn, jelly beans etc. Pretty neat the way they did it.

One leaflet started out with a message to, "OFFICERS AND MEN OF THE AMERICAN ARMY," and one was titled "CHRISTMAS – HOME – HAPPINESS" with a picture of a GI freezing to death and eating C-rations, plus a picture of a family getting ready to sit down to a wonderful Christmas turkey dinner. Boy, what a bunch of bull shit, and that is just how most of us took it. Both pictures became famous and were used in many US newspapers and magazines.

About this time, Cpl. John Cole, our loader, had been transferred from the company. I'm don't recall whether he was being rotated home or just transferred to another outfit, but we got a young black kid named Williams as his replacement.

Williams was new to combat, freshly from the States, but he seemed to be a good guy and seemed to know his position. Everyone in the tank seemed to accept him and I believe we all got to like him. He was with us on a couple raids and did a good job on loading the big gun. However, he was with us only a few weeks before he got transferred out to another unit. The loader's position was the only position in our tank that got rotated all during the time I was tank commander of Tank 22 (Doris). I don't know why, but we seemed to be a training tank loaders for the next few months, because we had two more loaders assigned to our tank during that time.

SSgt. Bob Baxter, Driver of Tank 26 and SFC Dennis Ottley playing around in the snow...

The 14th Infantry Regiment soldiers loaded up on our tanks, ready to moveout - Destination Yalu River, but orders canceled just before moving out...

Navy's Vought F4U Corsair was used during World War II where it earned an out-standing combat record. The Corsair had a distinctive sound to it that earned it the nick-name of "Whistling Death" by the Japanese. It was one of the fastest conventional type pursuit flyers used during WW II and it was one of the only non-jet planes used during the Korea War.

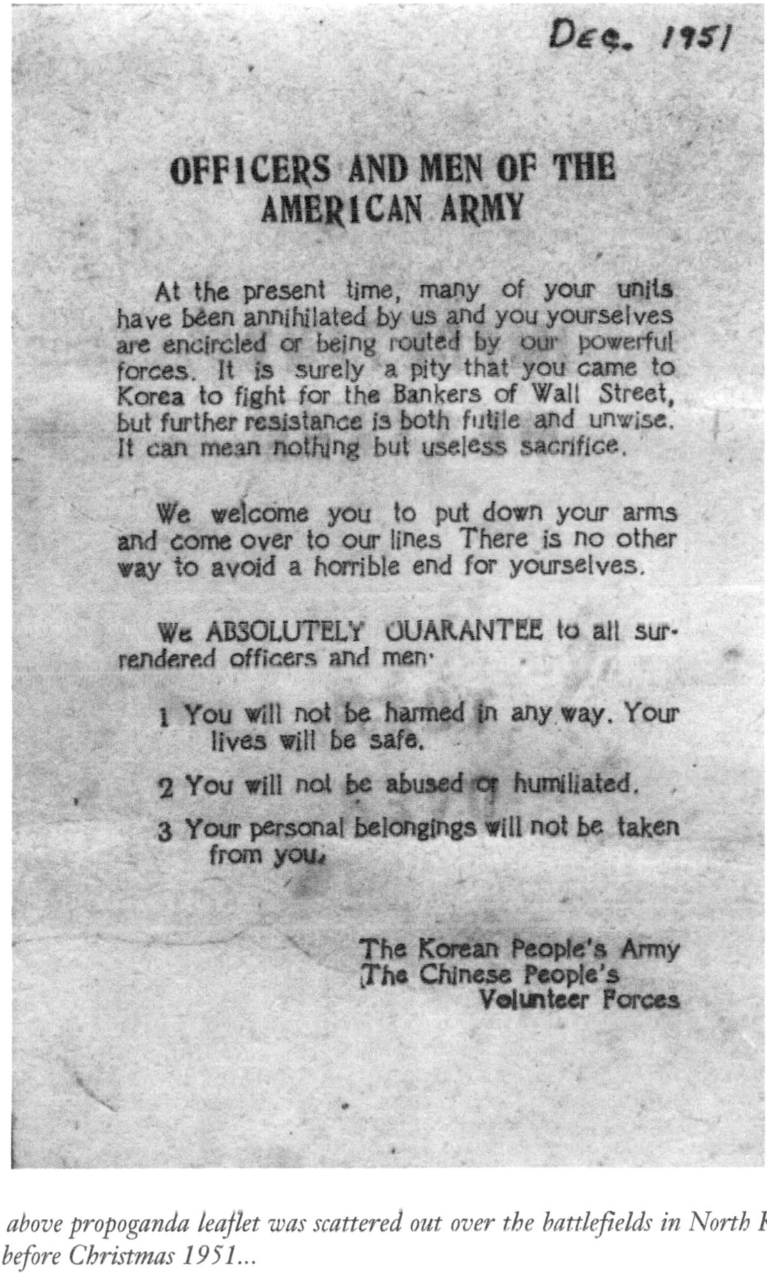

DEC. 1951

OFFICERS AND MEN OF THE AMERICAN ARMY

At the present time, many of your units have been annihilated by us and you yourselves are encircled or being routed by our powerful forces. It is surely a pity that you came to Korea to fight for the Bankers of Wall Street, but further resistance is both futile and unwise. It can mean nothing but useless sacrifice.

We welcome you to put down your arms and come over to our lines. There is no other way to avoid a horrible end for yourselves.

We ABSOLUTELY GUARANTEE to all surrendered officers and men:

1 You will not be harmed in any way. Your lives will be safe.

2 You will not be abused or humiliated.

3 Your personal belongings will not be taken from you.

The Korean People's Army
The Chinese People's
Volunteer Forces

The above propoganda leaflet was scattered out over the battlefields in North Korea just before Christmas 1951...

KOREA: DEC. 1951

CHRISTMAS —
HOME —
HAPPINESS —

Those who love you want you back home, safe and sound.

FIND A WAY OUT!

It's No Disgrace To Quit Fighting
In
This Unjust War!

Frozen rations eaten on the run.
Any moment he may have to run again,
to fight or die — and so may you.

This propoganda leaflet was folded up real tight and tied to a small bag of candy and then scattered out over the battlefields just before Christmas - 1951...

CHAPTER 19

A MERRY CHRISTMAS FROM THE NORTH

It was Christmas Eve. It was a cold night, but the sky was clear. We wouldn't be getting any snow this night. The temperature must have been zero or less, because it was damn cold. There was about a foot of snow on the ground, and I was up on our tank standing guard duty, trying to keep as warm as possible. With the tanks having no heaters, it was pretty difficult.

It was also a dark night, but the stars were out and the sky looked clear. While standing up there in my tank, I started thinking about my family back in the States and what they would be doing about now, but then I got to thinking that tonight wouldn't be Christmas Eve for them because of the full day change when we crossed the International Date Line.

Standing guard, I was watching out over the area, trying not to stare at one spot too long, because it makes things appear like they are moving and it can get a little scary. So, I tried to focus on the entire area, coming back to things that might look suspicious.

While standing there, all of a sudden, a bright line of fire appeared over my head. Our quad-50s in the rear started firing at the enemy with .50-caliber tracer bullets, making a line of fire light up almost directly over our heads. When it started, it kind of startled me. I guess the quad-50 crew just wanted to tell the enemy Merry Christmas. It only went on for 30 minutes or so, then they quit. Now things appeared to be pretty quiet and not much seemed to be going on.

Then, all of a sudden, I heard a whistling sound come over my head; knowing exactly what that was, I ducked down in the tank. Immediately looking up, I noticed it hit just about ten feet from our bunker. At that time, I jumped out of the tank and yelled to the crew to wake up and get moving.

They came running out of the bunker about the time another round hit close by. After hitting the ground, we all got up, jumped in our tank, and started moving it around the area, so they wouldn't have an easy target.

This went on almost all through the night. We were all in the tank, driving back and forth, moving around and around, hoping and praying that a shell didn't hit our tank or our bunker. The shelling stopped just before daylight.

After waiting for daylight to make sure there was no more artillery coming in, we parked the tank back in position and looked around to see if there was much damage. All we could see was a bunch of places where the shells landed and roughed up the ground a little and some brush was destroyed, but looking further, we spotted where our bunker had been hit. Apparently, the shell went through the edge of the roof of our bunker and into the ground where it ended up. Immediately, we knew it was probably a dud, so we called Lt. Epps over to look at it. When he arrived, he looked at where the bunker had been hit, and then he immediately called headquarters. He explained to them what had happened, and then he asked for a demolition team to be sent up.

When the team got there and after looking the situation over, they ordered us all back out of range and then proceeded to dig up the shell. After successfully digging the shell out of the ground, the team said that we were right, it was a dud. Their crew chief said, "You guys were damn lucky it didn't go off when it hit, because," he said, "it would have blown the bunker all to hell, and if you were in it at that time, some of you may not have made it through the night." We thanked them for getting the shell out of the ground and for the information.

We all got to talking about it and wondered whether that shell could have landed before we were all out of the bunker or after. It made a guy start thinking just what might have happened if it would have gone off while the crew was still in the bunker. I don't know of any GI that was over there ever hoping to get a Purple Heart. I know I sure as hell didn't want one, so I took my little black book out of my pocket and, once again, thanked God for keeping us all safe.

After the demolition crew left, the lieutenant talked to us a bit and said that they had gone through the same thing. So, I guess the North Koreans were throwing artillery at our entire platoon. I said to the lieutenant, "I guess that was the gooks' way of telling us Merry Christmas."

He kind of grinned and said, "Yeah I guess so, but I'm sure glad no one was hurt."

"Yeah," I said, "me, too."

Some of the other tank crews from the platoon had come over to see what was going on. After hearing about our little experience, they started talking about what happened at their locations. Apparently, they had all received enemy artillery through the night, but no damage was done and no one got

Our bunker before we were bombarded by enemy artillery on Christmas Eve, 1951

Our bunker was hit by a shell from enemy artillery on Christmas Eve, 1951. The top circle is where the shell went through the roof and the lower circle is where it went into the ground. It was a DUD, thank God...

hurt...thank God. I'm not sure what the gooks were trying to pull off, but maybe they just wanted to send us Christmas Cheer. They did.

• • •

'Twas the Night before Christmas in Korea – 1951...
Poem by the Author, Dennis J. Ottley

'Twas the night before Christmas on the Korean front,
Not a sound to be heard, not even a grunt.
Standing up in the turret of my Sherman tank,
Doing my guard duty like any good Yank.
Trying to stay warm with no heater to be had,
In a subzero cold winter, but a clear night, I'm glad.
When, all of a sudden, a bright line of fire appeared over my head.
It was friendly tracer bullets from quad-50s with hot lead.
While watching the bright line of fire, it caused me to blink.
I thought what if one shell falls short, I started to think.
I thought of my loved ones back home 8,000 miles away.
If they could see me now, what would they say?
I miss my family; my loving wife and my son most of all,
I only wish I had a phone, so I could make a Merry Christmas call.
All of a sudden, a loud whistle came over my head.
I knew what it was, I ducked down, I thought I was dead.
The round hit near, about ten feet from the bunker and all,
I jumped from my tank and warned my crew with a loud yelling call.
"Wake up, we're being attacked, grab your boots and your gear;
They're bombing us with artillery and some is landing near."
They jumped out of their fart-sacks, grabbing their boots and their stuff.
We all ran to the tank to move it around the area in a big huff.
We had to keep our tank moving to keep from getting hit.
The artillery from the north was coming in quite a bit.
The attack went on throughout this cold dreary night,
And the gooks quit firing just a while before daylight.
Looking around, we found no real damage had been done,
No one was hurt; thank you, God, nary a one.
While checking the area, we noticed our bunker had been hit.
Through the edge of the roof, into the ground the round had lit.
Only to find the round was a dud, and didn't go off, do tell.
Thanks again, God, it could have blown our bunker all to hell.

We called the lieutenant, he called the demolition crew, we were told.
They dug up the dud and said we were damn lucky it didn't explode.
We all went back to our duties, as good soldiers would.
The gooks had said Merry Christmas the only way they could.
This was a night to remember and a great story to be told,
We were all damn lucky during this weather of freezing cold.
Thanks to God no one was hurt through this long and fearful night.
'Twas the night before Christmas, a night long of fear and fright.

•   •   •

After the big night was over, sitting in my bunker, I got some of my recent letters from home and started to read a few. The Christmas package from my wife, Sandy, had just barely been opened, so I got it out and shared it with the rest of my crew. We all heated up our cups full of water and had some Lipton's dry soup that I had received in the package. We all said, "Merry Christmas," and enjoyed our soup.

After a while, sitting and thinking about what had happened, we all went outside and started cleaning and straightening up the mess that the gooks left us during the night. There wasn't much said about the incident all day long. I guess the crew was just not in the mood to be talking about it at this time. I think they were just thinking how damn lucky we all were and wishing to hell we were all back in the States and out of this damn hellhole, and thinking God for keeping us from being harmed.

On New Year's Eve, the gooks, once again, sent a few rounds of artillery over, but not so close, so we didn't get too concerned about it. This time, it only lasted until about midnight. No damage was done; none of the rounds landed anywhere nearby. I suppose they were just being a little friendly and wanting to help us celebrate our New Year. Thanks, but no thanks. We certainly didn't need any help from them.

Old Glory
A Poem by Dick Jenkins, of the 2nd Combat Engr. Bn., 2nd ID

The Korean dawn was breaking with the first hint of light,
As the detail was returning from a long, hard night.
The night had been savage, full of flashes and sounds,
The hills were still shaking from the impounding rounds.
They had lost their direction trying to find their way back,
And still weren't sure they were on the right track.

While they struggled on back, the sounds grew dim,
As they climbed each hill to the top of the rim.
As they got to the top and crested the last hill,
The heart rending view stays with them still.
They had made it back 'home' as they all knew,
For across the wide valley 'OLD GLORY' flew.

CHAPTER 20

BACK TO RESERVE, A DRUNK,

AND A LONG, COLD RIDE

The entire 25th Infantry Division, except the Tank Company of the 14th Infantry Regiment, had been relieved from the front lines just before Christmas. The 14th hadn't been relieved until after New Year's Day. The 25th was relieved by the 2nd Infantry Division and then moved back into a reserve area near Kapyong. There, the division was engaged in training activities and in maintaining the secondary defensive line.

We were all happy to be back in reserve where we could all take a rest, but the second night we were back, one of the soldiers in the platoon got a hold of a couple of bottles of Canadian Club Whiskey. I don't know whether he got it from some GI that had just got off R & R, or from the Turks or Greeks, but he had it. He invited a bunch of us over to his squad tent to celebrate being in reserve. To make a long story short, we all got pretty damn drunk, myself included. I got sicker than hell and had one of the worst hangovers that a person should have to have. I believe the party was all over by 10:00 P.M., when most of us turned in.

The next morning when they called for the troops to fall in for roll call and calisthenics, there was a bunch of us with hangovers, including a couple of the platoon sergeants. After our drills, we went to the mess hall for breakfast, but by this time, most of us were feeling a little better. So, we ate and then just spent the rest of the day cleaning and fixing up the area. There were no more parties or drinking for any of us after that night, except for a beer once in a while.

Most of the time, while in reserve, we went through a lot of training. We participated with the infantry by going on several mock raids and assaults, involving various hills behind the front. We also had many classes on map reading, weaponry, combat tactics and strategies, and other means, plus, of course, we went through our usual calisthenics each morning before breakfast.

The one thing about being in reserve, besides being safer, was that the chow was much better and we had chow at least twice a day. Believe it or not, it actually was pretty damn good food, regardless of all the bitching that was done by the troops. I believe most of it was just something to bitch about and to give the mess sergeant a bad time, because it wasn't that bad. I thought that we had a pretty good cook as our mess sergeant.

While in reserve, we did a lot of card playing, such as poker and blackjack. I did pretty well playing blackjack, but I lost my butt in poker. So, I spent most of my leisure time reading and just playing blackjack. Sandy often sent me books to read, such as the Mike Hammer series by Mickey Spillane and a few westerns. I enjoyed reading them, especially the western stories.

It felt pretty good to be out of the actual combat for a while. Being back in reserve gave us a chance to see some of our buddies other than those in our platoon. I had the opportunity to visit with some of my friends from Wyoming. We were able to get together and talk about what we had heard from back home and our different combat stories while on the front. This was the first time that I had heard anything about SFC Ray Tanner, commander of Tank 43, hitting an anti-tank mine during a raid. He got a slight wound out of it, but nothing that the medics couldn't take care of. He was actually ashamed to accept the Purple Heart, but he had no choice.

While visiting with the rest of my buddies from Wyoming, I found out that they all had been on the front, going through similar operations that we had gone through. They all indicated that no one had been hurt or badly wounded, but a couple of them had also lost their tanks by anti-tank mines. So, we did have a few stories to exchange.

It was especially good to see my closest buddy from Wyoming, SFC Boyd Henderson. His wife, Beverly, and my wife were also good friends back in Evanston, so we had a lot to talk about. We exchanged stories about what we had heard about, things that had happened back home, and how the kids were all doing. Things like that. Boyd was a good friend and we kind of watched out for each other when we could. He had spent four years in the Marine Corps before joining the Wyoming National Guard. He was about four years older than I was.

I remember when one of the GIs in our outfit came up to me one day and asked me if he could read one of my letters. I don't recall his name, but he was in the same platoon as I was, but with another tank. Apparently he never got any mail at all, so he came to me. He asked me if I would mind him reading one of my letters. He said that he didn't get any mail and that he would like to just see how it feels to read a letter from the States. I asked him, "Why don't you get any mail from home?" In answering, he stated that as far as he knew, he had no one; he had no family that he knew about. After asking him why and what had happened, he didn't seem to know much. It was like him having amnesia all those years, but I didn't push him much. I just told him that my letters were kind of personal and that I wasn't sure that I wanted anyone else reading them.

But, after listening to him for a while, I got to feeling sorry for him. So, I gave in and let him read the latest letter that I had received from my wife, Sandy. While reading it, he looked like he was about to cry, and then I really felt sorry for him. I was glad that I had let him read it. I never had run into anyone like him before, but he thanked me for it and handed the letter back. He assured me that he would not tell anyone that he read it, and then he left, not saying much. He was an alright guy, but kind of mysterious.

I didn't tell anyone about him or about what had happened until I was rotated out and on my way home. Then I told some of my buddies from Wyoming while on the ship. They told me that they knew him and knew that he didn't have any family and knew he didn't get any mail. I guess everyone that knew him kind of felt sorry for him.

While we were in reserve, our platoon hired a young Korean boy (boy-san) as our houseboy that we called Joe. We called him Joe because that was what he wanted to be called. I don't recall his real name, but it seemed that most of the Korean boy-sans wanted to be called Joe because of being related to the term GI Joe. Young Joe would clean up our tents and wash our clothes down at the nearby creek on rocks. He also helped keep the area clean and ran errands for us. We each paid him one dollar a month, which came to about $19 or $20 a month to him. That was pretty good pay back then for a Korean boy. He thought he was in high heaven getting that kind of money, but he always took it home and gave it to his folks. He seemed like a good kid, but a lot of the Koreans would steal from you if they got the chance. You couldn't really blame them for it, though. It was all a matter of survival to them. From what I saw of them, I always felt that the Koreans were basically pretty good people, they were just going through some pretty tough times, trying to survive.

I had it happen to me. Just before leaving our reserve area for the Mundung-ni Valley, I had my shaving kit stolen by a boy-san while we were loading up our tanks. It had my safety razor and all my toilet articles in it. I had an idea who took it, but I didn't say anything. I just figured he needed it worse than I did; I could always replace it, which I did, but it was an inconvenience.

A lot of the Korean men (papa-sans) would cut our hair for about twenty-five cents each time while in reserve. It was hard to keep our hair cut, but between some of our buddies and the papa-sans we were able to get by. I never saw anyone get a shave by someone else. I think most of the time we just shaved ourselves, using our helmets for a wash basin. I don't recall anyone with a beard, a mustache maybe, but no beard.

While up front, Lt. Epps cut my hair until he got in the accident, and then we just started cutting each other's hair. Sometimes, we ended up with a haircut that looked pretty shabby, but like they say, there are only a couple weeks between a good haircut and a bad one.

During this time, headquarters had set up a class for a bunch of us to attend at a location about 20 or so miles to the west. I don't recall the name of the location, but it was quite a distance away from where we were located. The class had something to do with leadership, because the only non-coms (NCOs - non-commissioned officers) that were scheduled to go were tank commanders, including Lt. Epps. The lieutenant was to be our chaperone and assist the driver in finding the location.

Some of the tank commanders that were chosen to go, besides myself, were SFCs Boyd Henderson, Ray Tanner, Verd Erickson, and Don Johnson, all from Wyoming. There were others, but I don't recall who they were. There were about eight or ten of us, if I remember right.

This was the longest and coldest ride that any of us had ever gone through. All of us non-coms were in the back of the truck, while Lt. Epps and the driver were in the cab where it was warm. All we had on, other than our long johns, were our field jackets. We left our parkas at camp, not thinking we would need them. We thought that we would be there in just a few hours. The roads in Korea weren't built for fast traveling, so we figured it would take a little time. But boy, were we ever in for an awakening.

We left camp that morning fairly early and never reached our destination. Apparently, our driver got lost and Lt. Epps didn't seem to know where we were to be going, either. Maybe, they just lost their bearings all together, because we rode in the back of that truck for hours and hours, not knowing where in the hell we were at. We were damn lucky that we didn't get into enemy territory, because we weren't very far from the front lines.

We went over hill after hill, trying to find the place we were supposed to be at, but we never made it. When Epps and the driver figured it was too late to make the class, they decided to head back, but ended up getting lost again. Thank God it was a clear night, but the temperature was below zero after the sun went down and it turned dark. The driver felt pretty bad and was really embarrassed, but that didn't help keep us warm. We were freezing back in the bed of the truck. The truck did have a canvas cover over the back, but there was nothing else to keep us warm. Amazingly, the guys never got mad or did much bitching, but we were sure anxious to get back to our camp.

By the time we got back, it was pretty late and we were a bunch of frozen and hungry GIs. The mess hall was closed, so all we got to eat was food that we had received from home or our C-rations, but that was alright; I think we were more tired that hungry, anyway. We never got to the class we were supposed to go to, but we really didn't give a damn. We were just damn glad to be back.

It was now January 28, 1952, my twentieth birthday. Wasn't much going on, but everyone seemed to know that it was my birthday. They all came around and wished me happy birthday, but no biggie, mostly just another day. However, I did get a couple of packages from home with more food and some more clothing—socks, underwear, and such. Under the circumstances, getting those packages and a happy birthday from home was plenty.

I remember when I was in reserve, I saw an advertisement in a magazine that one of my buddies had received. This ad was from Frederick's of Hollywood, advertising a beautiful dress that I thought would look nice on my wife, Sandy. So, I thought that I would send for it and have it sent directly to Sandy. I was pretty naïve about women's clothes and their sizes at that time, but I wanted to surprise her.

I knew my wife's waist size was about 22, so I ordered a size 22 dress for her. When she received it and tried it on, it was three times too big. She wrote back and said the dress was way too big and that it should have been about a size 8. She said everyone got quite a laugh out of it. I thought *how stupid can a guy be?* I just thought if her waist was 22 inches, why wouldn't that be the dress size? But, I was wrong. She sent it back.

It wasn't long after we got back in reserve we lost our loader again—PFC Williams, the black kid that had joined our crew as loader a few weeks prior. I never did hear why he was transferred, but this time, we got an American Indian to replace him. I don't recall his name, but if I remember right, he was from Oklahoma of the Cherokee Nation. He was also a great guy and seemed to know what he was doing, but he wasn't with us very long, only a couple weeks.

We were now into the latter part of February when we heard that the 25th Division would be receiving orders very soon to go back up on the line. It was nice while it lasted being back in reserve, but we knew it wouldn't last long. Our new orders indicated that we would be moving further to the east to an area called Mundung-ni, completely different than where we had been.

One of the soldiers in the 2nd platoon getting a haircut by a Korean man (pap-san) while in reserve...

On the left is the 2nd platoon standing at ease in formation. SFC Dennis Ottley circled. MSgt. James, platoon sergeant standing in front of platoon...

SFC Dennis Ottley with the platoon's house boy (boy-san), we called him Joe...

SSgt. Troy Griffith (left) and SSgt. Harry Gray (right), both tank drivers. Gray was Ottley's driver of Tank 22...

SFC Dennis Ottley (left) and SFC Boyd Henderson (right) standing next to regiment sign at our reserve area...

SFC Ottley (left) and SFC Ray Tanner (right) at our reserve area...

CHAPTER 21

MUNDUNG-NI VALLEY

On February 23, 1952, the 25th Division returned to the front line near Mundung-ni, northeast of the Hwach'on Reservoir. There, we resumed the front line routine of patrols, ambushes, artillery exchanges, and bunker maintenance. The division also secured and defended forward outposts beyond the MLR (main line of resistance). Again, we were the first platoon out of the Tank Company to be ordered back to the front with Tank 22 to set up in a blocking position.

When we arrived to our position, we noticed that there was already a bunker built. This made us happy because it was still pretty cold out, and the ground was still frozen, making it tough to fill sand bags. Before we got here, we all thought that the first thing we would have to do was build another bunker, so this was a good surprise to find out there was one already in place.

Our crew consisted of the same old bunch, except for our new loader. PFC Harvey Neumann was assigned to our tank a week or so before we moved to the Mundung-ni area. If I remember right, he was from Illinois; not sure, but he ended up being a good crew member, and everyone seemed to like him.

Mundung-ni Valley is an area where, in the previous year, some very intense fighting went on. In the northerly end on the valley, there were still several American tanks sitting that had been destroyed by the enemy. They were burned and destroyed so badly that it was senseless to pull them out, so they just left them there. We were told that several of the tankers had been killed and burned alive. Also, several had been severely wounded. That may be one reason the infantry called tanks "iron coffins."

Our location was right across the valley from a hill that the GIs called Dagmar, after a famous actress named Dagmar. She was well known during

186

the 1940s and 50s, mostly for her large breasts. The hill Dagmar, I don't recall the actual number of the hill, had two large peaks that resembled a pair of a woman's large boobs, so like the actress, they called the hill Dagmar. There was also a hill in the area called Jane Russell that the GIs named for the same reason. There were quite a few of the hills in Korea to which the GIs gave similar nicknames.

The hill Dagmar was only about 200 or 300 hundred yards across the valley from our position. We were so close that you could see by the naked eye North Korean troops walking around near their bunkers and in their trenches. It seemed like we were much closer to the enemy in this position than we were over in the Kumhwa and the Iron Triangle areas.

About three days after we had set up position at Mundung-ni, the peace talks at Panmunjom appeared to be getting closer to an armistice. Because of that, a cease-fire order came down from headquarters. The order was directed to both sides. It included all of the United Nation armies and the enemy, both the North Korean and Chinese Reds. This meant neither side should fire on one another, but, in some cases, that didn't seem to matter much.

Not too long after the order came out, a small platoon of the 14th Infantry Regiment was sent north across the front line for nothing but a reconnaissance mission to check out an area. When they attempted to cross the dry river bed that ran down the middle of the valley just in front of us, they were ambushed and fired upon by the gooks. While the platoon was trying to retreat, they returned the fire, killing two gooks that we could see lying in the river bed. During the attack, the platoon lost two that had been killed and a few wounded.

We heard that after the platoon got back to their position, carrying two dead soldiers and helping the wounded, the lieutenant in charge of the detail was really pissed off, because of the cease-fire order, and said he would like to take the two dead and throw them in the General's lap and tell him what a phony order the cease-fire was. No one could blame him, because nobody liked the order in the first place. Most of troops were pretty upset about it right from the start. It didn't help the morale of the troops much.

The next day, when Cpl. Ted Davis was setting up in the turret of our tank, he spotted a large group of gooks walking down the trench on the hill Dagmar. He called me up there to take a look and, sure enough, they were like he said. Davis seemed very anxious to fire on them with the .50-caliber machine gun and asked me if he could, but I told him that the cease-fire order was still on and that we wouldn't be allowed to fire on them. He was a little upset, especially after what had happened to the platoon the day before. I finally told him that I would call the lieutenant and see if we could get permission. So I did, but it didn't do any good. Lt. Epps told me just what I thought

187

he would. He told me that we definitely could not open fire on them, and that the order still stood. Davis was really upset and said, "What the hell kind of a war is this?" The rest of us just thought it.

A few days passed and those two dead gooks lying in the river bed were still there. They appeared to be very black and bloated. We thought that was kind of strange, because most any other time, you would have thought that the gooks would have removed them. They were still there when we left our position a few weeks later.

While in a blocking position at the front, the mess truck brought up our chow, as always. They parked the truck about midway between all the troops in the area, causing us to have to walk a couple hundred feet or so for our grub, which no one griped about; we just wanted to eat. It was either that or C-rations.

When our crew went for their chow, we always took turns, leaving at least four crew members on the tank. There's one particular day that I really remember. On this day, I happened to be the last of my crew to go get my grub, so when my turn came, I walked in the direction of the truck. You couldn't see the mess truck from our tank. It was parked on the other side of a hill behind us.

After loading up my mess gear with my food and my coffee cup with coffee, I started walking back to our position. After walking a ways, I heard a whistling sound and knowing what it was, I hit the dirt. Before getting up, I looked over to my left rear about 30 or so feet away where it had landed. What I saw really surprised me. I noticed right away that it was a WP (white phosphorus) round. I then said to myself, "What the hell? I have never seen the gooks throw a WP round at us, it's got to be from our side." I knew that it was WP because of the white-yellowish vapor it let off. Knowing a little about white phosphorus, I laid there for a few minutes knowing that if that stuff gets on you it can burn. Before getting up, I looked down at my mess gear, figuring that I may have to go back to the truck for more food, but being surprised that I hadn't lost a bit of my food, but I did lose about half of my coffee. So, I was happy that I didn't have to go back. I got up and continued back to my tank.

When I got back, I told the crew about what had happened. They agreed that it was probably a friendly round coming from behind us because the cease-fire order was still on and the gooks wouldn't just be firing one round, they would fire at least three or four rounds. We decided that the artillery had either fired a round and it went short, or they were just goofing off and accidently fired a round. We never did find out, but no other rounds were fired after that one.

We were now into March and the weather was starting to warm up. The ground was starting to thaw, causing the area to get real muddy and sloppy, making it a little hard to get around, but we were managing to keep our equipment and weapons in good shape. The worst part was when it was chow time and having to go to the mess truck through the mud to get our food and then walking back, but it was better than eating C-rations. The cease-fire order was still on, so we didn't have to worry too much about any artillery coming in, causing us to need to hit the ground. That would have been a bit messy in this mud. About this Time, Lt. Epps gave us the word that we were going to be replaced and sent back to the reserve area for a while. He said we would be replaced by the 4th Platoon of the Tank Company. At this time, the cease-fire order had been removed and it appeared that the war was back on.

The tank and crew that replaced us and took over our position, surprisingly, just happened to be Tank 42 of the 4th Platoon, the tank on which my best friend SFC Boyd Henderson was tank commander. I was glad to see him again after being on the front for that past few weeks. It was great to have the chance to visit with him and talk to him for a short time about things back home, but in a few minutes, we had to get in our tank and leave. As we left, we wished them the best of luck and told them to stay safe, that we hoped to be seeing them again soon.

But, being that the cease-fire order was now called off and the war was back on line, the 4th Platoon was in a much more dangerous situation than we were. In fact, it was just a few days after we left that they were fired on by enemy artillery. During this barrage, Boyd had got hit in the leg by shrapnel as he was diving for cover. They brought him back to reserve to the medics to have his leg looked at. When I heard he had been wounded, not knowing just how bad it was, I was quite concerned until I saw him. He was treated by the medics and released. Then he was sent back to the front to his tank and crew.

It was just a couple days when Lt. Epps came and talked to me about a new assignment. He said that our crew had been selected to immediately report to a location on Heartbreak Ridge, and that we would be told what our assignment was when we got there.

The above photos are of hills and area across from our position at Mundung-ni Valley. The hills are occupied with North Koreans and you could see them by the naked eye. That is how close we are to them.

This photo is of the hill called Dagmar. It is the hill right across the valley from our positon at Mundung-ni. It is full of gooks...

This photo is of Mundung-ni Valley looking northerly. Note the small village in the center...

SFC Boyd Henderson (left) and SFC Dennis Ottley (right), both Tank Commanders, standing next to Tank 22, Ottley's tank...

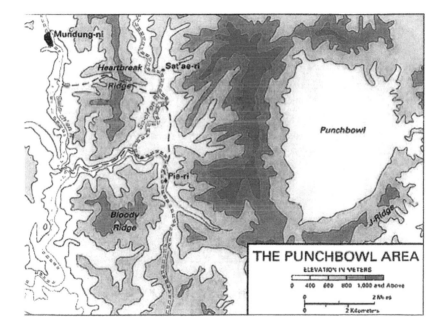

Mundung-ni

Heartbreak
Ridge

Sat'ae-ri

Punchbowl

Pia-ri

Bloody
Ridge

J-Ridge

THE PUNCHBOWL AREA

ELEVATION IN METERS

0   400   600   800   1,000 and Above

2 Miles

2 Kilometers

CHAPTER 22

HEARTBREAK RIDGE

Going back to my squad tent, after talking to the lieutenant, I told my crew what I knew about our new assignment. I told them that the lieutenant couldn't tell us much, only that we were being assigned to a position up on Hill 851 (Heartbreak Ridge) to participate and support a reinforced platoon from the 14ᵗʰ Infantry Regiment, and that we would not be taking our tank "Doris" with us. It would stay parked in the motor pool until we got back. Lt. Epps wasn't sure how long we would be there, but an M4 Sherman tank and a bunker was already in place, waiting for us, and that we were going up on top of the ridge, but didn't know the exact location.

He said that we were just one of two tank crews out of the entire company chosen for this assignment, and said that we all should feel honored to have been chosen. Also, he said we would receive more instructions when we got there, and that we had to be ready to leave early tomorrow morning, that a truck would be waiting for us. Apparently, this was a mission that they were trying to keep a little quiet at the time. I didn't get much sleep that night, wondering just what the hell we were getting into, and I don't suppose the rest of the crew did, either.

After getting all our gear together, we left that morning on the truck. We were heading to a location somewhere on top of Hill 851 (Heartbreak Ridge) where, in the past, there had been some pretty severe battles fought.

It seemed like it was taking a long time to get there, but it was all uphill and slow going. As we arrived at our location, the first thing I saw was the Sherman tank that we were to use while we were there. Looking around, I could understand why the tank was still there and why we didn't bring our own tank. We were up on the mountain pretty high and I don't know of any driver that would have cared to have the job of driving that tank down the hill. I'm sure they would have tried, but I guess the decision was to just leave it up there. Hell, as far as I know, that tank could still be there after all these years.

We unloaded our gear and set up house in our new bunker. The bunker was quite different than what we had been used to; this bunker was cut into the hillside and built out toward the road. The road went past the front of the bunker and ended about 40 or 50 feet to the edge of the ridge. After getting all settled in, we checked our tank over and then just waited for the group to come and give us our instructions.

When those in charge got there, they told us that we would be there for two or three weeks; that it depended on how things went. They told us that a night assault on an area being held by the Chinese Reds was being planned, and that a reinforced platoon of infantry had been organized for the attack. They said it would definitely take place at night. They went on to tell us that in a few days, some instructors would come up to spend some time, helping us set up our targets and firing schedule. We would be firing on different targets, targets that were out of our sight and we would have to zero in on the designated targets and get all our bearings set up during the daytime.

They said that some instructors would be there to direct us on setting up the different targets, and that they would designate what targets we would be firing at. They told us that a forward observer would be in place to direct us on the targets, because we wouldn't be able to see them even in the daylight. The observer would be with us during the practice time, setting up the targets, and during the real thing. He would be doing this by radio, instructing where and when to fire. The targets would be numbered and we would be firing on them in the order we were instructed.

We were to fire on targets that we couldn't even see in the daytime, let alone at night. This was going to be something new for our crew. We all thought that this kind of firing was for the artillery, not for the tankers, but we managed it. We had never been involved in any type of night fighting, until now. This would be a first for all of us, and that is why we had to mark our targets during the day. They said that we would be told the time and date later, but right now, it depended on the timing of when everyone was ready, that they would let us know in plenty of time.

They also told us that the ammo truck would be coming up soon with a load of HE (high explosive) 76 mm rounds that we would be using. We were to load our tank to its capacity with the ammo, and after we got through getting our practice shooting over with, they would send the truck up again before the real thing came off.

The tank radio wasn't working and that's why we had the radio in the bunker. They said that once the driver and his assistant had pulled the tank up to the edge of the ridge they would dismount, and then they would go to the bunker and get on the radio for instructions. At that time, we would be told over the radio what target to fire on, how fast to fire, and when to start and stop firing. The driver and his assistant would relay those instructions from the bunker to us in the tank.

They said the commander, the gunner, and the loader would have to stay in the tank with all hatches buttoned down tight and when anyone dismounted from the tank, they were to use what we called the belly hatch or trap door at the bottom of the tank. They said this was for our own safety, because we would surely be getting bombarded with mortar shells and maybe some heavy artillery.

I asked how we were to communicate with the driver and his assistant while they were on the ground and we were all buttoned up. They said that the loader was to keep his porthole (sometimes called a pistol port) opened at all times, so we could hear what the instructions were from the ground. The porthole is on the left side of the turret. It is an opening about 6 x 8 inches in size and has a small door with a lever that opens and closes it. It is located on the loader's side of the turret. It would be on the side of the tank facing the bunker. It is an opening that is used for many different purposes.

The mess truck was coming up each day, plus a jeep would bring the mail up every couple days, and also pick up the outgoing mail. The mess truck would only come part way up the hill, where we would have to walk down about the length of a football field to get to it. Going down wasn't too bad, coming back was quite a walk, but it was good exercise. The mail jeep came all the way up to our bunker, but we had to back the tank down the hill a few feet to meet the ammo truck, so we could load the tank with the 76 mm shells. Thank God we didn't have to carry the ammo very far.

While we were waiting for the instructors to come up and set us up on our firing schedule, we didn't do much of anything, except work on the tank, read books, write letters, and take a few pictures with our cameras. We also took turns taking guard duty. When the tank was not in action, we always pulled it back to the bunker out of sight of the enemy, but we still had to have someone on guard duty every night.

We also got a chance to talk to a few of the infantry troops and see how they were doing. As far as I heard, nothing was said about the plan among the troops. Everyone just seemed to keep hush, hush about it, but you could tell that they were all kinds of worried of what was ahead. Again, I was glad I was a tanker. I just had a feeling that these guys were in for a tough battle, but I hoped to hell that everything would go smoothly for all of us and not too many would get hurt.

We were told that it would be the Chinese Communists that we would be battling this time. This would be a little different from what we had been used to; we had never been up against them before. Someone said there was a big difference between the North Koreans and the Chinese. They said the Chinese were more civilized and more rational than the North Koreans. That you never knew for sure what the North Koreans were going to do, but you could pretty well predict what the Chinese would do. I don't think that made anyone feel much better, but I guess it gave them something to think about.

The instructors finally came back to assist us in setting up our targets. They stayed with us all the time while directing us to what targets and locations we would be firing on. They said that everyone would be synchronizing their watches sometime just before the big battle started to make sure that everyone was working on the exact same time, right down to the split second, because if anyone involved in the program was off on their timing even a little bit, it could cause problems. They said the entire plan was based on timing and depended on everyone being right on schedule. We all had military watches that were known to keep excellent time.

The instructors spent a good part of the next few days with us explaining the plan of action and setting us on our firing schedule. They had us firing on various targets, writing down on paper all of our bearings—ranges, scopes etc. The forward observer with his binoculars was assisting us with setting up the targets. They went over the entire program with us several times to make sure that we were ready for the big event. They finally left, feeling very confident that we knew what we were doing and that we could get the job done with no flaws.

Days later, we got the order that the assault was to start immediately that night and for us to get ready and get our tank in place. We had the order to synchronize our watches, and be ready to start as soon as we got the go-ahead. As tankers firing in the dark, we had to know the exact time to start and when to stop. If we weren't exact on our time, we could very well cause a lot of casualties on the wrong side.

So, dark came and we all got the order to get set. Grey, our driver, had his assistant Davis help direct him while he pulled the tank up to the edge of the ridge, so he didn't get too far out. After getting the tank in place, Grey dismounted through the belly hatch. Blades, Neumann, and I mounted the tank and then buttoned the hatches up tight. We were now setup, waiting for orders to do our part. Grey brought us our first order, which was to fire on a designated target given to us by a number. We were to fire a round every fifteen seconds, starting at a certain synchronized time. The time came and we started firing. I said to Blades and Neumann, "I hope we don't have to fire at this speed for very long; it may get the barrel so hot, causing it to drop." They agreed, but after a few minutes, the order was to slow down to 30 seconds. That was still firing quite fast and I was a little concerned about the barrel getting too hot, but after a while, they slowed us down again. The rest of the night, we fired in different intervals at different targets as we were ordered.

I was concerned about the gun barrel getting too hot, because when I was in the States training, we had that happen to one of our tanks. Out on the firing range, one of our tankers fired too fast, too long, causing the barrel to get so hot it fell and caused the rounds to hit way short. So, I knew it could happen and so did the rest of my crew.

All the time we were firing on the enemy, they were throwing mortar rounds at us. Some rounds exploded around the area near the bunker and some actually hit our tank. We had four or five mortar rounds land and explode on top of the turret right over our heads. It sounded like heavy rocks dropping and shattering on top of the turret. We figured that it had to be Chinese 82 or 83 mm mortar shells that they were firing at us. Heavier artillery would have done much more damage. What worried us most was the fact that they had our range, and that they might start throwing heavier stuff at us. Heavier artillery could have done some real damage to the tank.

The driver and his assistant stayed in the bunker as much as they could because of the mortar shells hitting close by. When they had to relay a message to us, they would run out of the bunker to the tank and give us the message and run back, sometimes having to fall and dodge the shells that were coming in. Thank God they never got hurt.

The shells hitting the tank weren't doing any damage, so we just tried to ignore them and kept firing our gun as we were instructed. It seemed like we had been firing for hours before they finally slowed the intervals down to about every ten or fifteen minutes. At last, they slowed us down to about every half hour or so, until the attack was over.

The assault was finally over about an hour or two before daylight. After staying in our positions for a while, Blades and Neumann left the tank through the belly hatch. I was just about ready to dismount when I heard voices outside the tank. It was still dark out when I heard someone come up to our tank and tell the crew that the battle was all over and that our boys took one hell of a beating. I could hear them through the porthole.

I heard one of the soldiers, a lieutenant I was told, ask my crew if they could go down below where the wounded were and help get them out. Grey told them that they would have to talk to the commander, Sgt. Ottley. At that time, Grey came over to the porthole of the turret and said, "Sarg, the lieutenant here wants to know if we can go down and help get the wounded out."

I said, "How bad was it?" and Grey replied, "Pretty damn bad, I guess."

After thinking for a minute, I said, "Tell him that we would like to, but we are not allowed to leave our tank. If we leave it and something happened, we would be in big trouble."

Grey said, "Okay, I will tell him." Grey came back and told me that the lieutenant said that he understood and thanked us and left.

I could hear the crew still outside the tank talking to other GIs when I decided to get out of the tank myself. At this time I did something real stupid, not thinking. I could see no sense of dismounting by way of the belly hatch when everything seemed to be over, so I threw my top hatch open and jumped out real fast, forgetting that the engine deck would have dozens of empty brass shells laying on it from firing the gun. When I jumped out, I tripped over the empty brass, causing me to trip and fall off the tank, hitting one of the soldiers to whom the crew was talking. My head hit his helmet and knocked me colder than hell for a moment or two. The crew helped me into the bunker, where I cleared my head and told my crew, "I guess I should have used the belly hatch like the rest of you. I forgot all about the empty brass on the deck. Boy, what a stupid thing to do," I said.

Grey agreed and said, "What were you trying to do, get a Purple Heart?"

I said, "No way, I didn't come over here for a Purple Heart." They all agreed and kind of chuckled.

I then asked the crew how the lieutenant took it when I told him we couldn't leave the tank. The crew said he seemed to agree with me and said he understood and thanked us and left. They said that from what everyone had indicated, the reinforced platoon they sent in to take the area ran into about a thousand Chinese troops and got slaughtered. I said, "That is too bad, the Chinese must have known about the attack, or at least expected something was coming. I went on to say, "I sure would have liked to have helped them with the wounded, though, but you all know what would have happened to us if we had left our tank."

"Yeah," Grey said, "we would have been called on it, that's for sure." They all agreed that it was the right decision.

Waiting for daylight, we continued to talk a little about what had happened, and how badly we all felt about our troops taking such a beating. "Yeah," I said, "it's too bad that the attack didn't come off better, but I'm damn glad none of us were hurt," and took my little black book out of my left breast pocket and said, "Thank you, once again, God, for keeping us safe." My crew, not saying anything, just shook their heads in agreement.

Daylight came and after we stacked all the empty brass in a pile, Grey got in the driver's seat and backed the tank up even with the bunker, just out of sight of the enemy, and then we kind of straightened the area up a little, waiting for the mess truck. We were all kind of hungry. We had just been eating C-rations and what else we had on hand since the mess truck had left the day before. After eating chow and cleaning our mess gear, we all went to the bunker and got some rest. We were all pretty damn tired after being up all night, sitting in the tank, and attending to the radio.

That afternoon, the truck came to pick up the empty brass. We all pitched in, cleaning up the brass, and helping to load the truck. Not too long after the truck had left, we got orders that our assignment was over and we were to have our gear ready, that a truck would come to take us off the ridge the first thing the next morning. That was good news to us. I believe we were all pretty tired and anxious to get back to reserve. The rest of the evening, we talked a while longer, then hit the sack, but did take our turns at guard duty through the night.

That morning, we loaded up the truck with all our gear and came down off the ridge, leaving the tank up there. I don't know how long that tank had been up there, but it had probably been a while. When we got back to our camp, I was quite surprised to find that most of my Wyoming friends and some others were gone. They were on R & R (rest and relaxation, sometimes called rest and recuperation), and I would have been with them, if I hadn't been up on Heartbreak.

Lt. Epps came over to our squad tent to talk to us mostly about how things went up on the ridge. He first welcomed us back to camp. He said he was very anxious to get over here and talk to us about our assignment on Heartbreak. He said that from all reports, we had done a great job and carried out our mission very well. "However," he said, "the mission overall was not successful. Apparently, headquarters had underestimated the Chinese. They outnumbered our troops about 5 to 1, causing our troops to get slaughtered. But," he went on to say, "you tankers did your part very well and I'm damn proud of you and the company commander told me to tell you, 'Thanks and congratulations on such a great job,' and that he was also very proud of you."

I spoke up and said, "That's good to hear; we were kind of wondering if we did our part okay, being as the assault overall appeared to be a failure."

Then he asked us how we liked being up there on top of Heartbreak. We told him that it wasn't so bad, but sure different from what we had been used to. The training sessions setting up our targets and writing down all of our bearings, ranges, etc., we told him, got a little boring, but the night firing was different than what we had been used to. We told him that the night fighting was not only different, but it was a lot more frightening than daylight fighting, mainly because you couldn't see anything that was going on.

Then, we told him about the lieutenant, who we thought was infantry, wanting us to go down below where the battle was and help get the wounded out. We told him that we couldn't, that we sure would if we could, but we weren't allowed to leave our tank. The lieutenant said that we had done the right thing, and that we would probably have been in big trouble if we had left it, regardless of whether anything had happened to the tank or not. He said, "Under the code, you are not to leave your tank under any circumstances, unless it is on fire or damaged really bad, and you are under heavy fire."

The lieutenant stuck around, talking to us for about an hour, asking us questions, and filling us in to what had been happening with the company while we were up on the ridge. He said they pulled the 14th Infantry Regiment, including the tank company, off the front lines for a while. In our conversation, we told him how we had to get in and out of the tank and about the tank not having a radio. We told him about the bunker and the mortar shells hitting our tank and around our area. We asked him a few questions on why our outfit was pulled back. He said we had been replaced by an outfit that hadn't been up there, yet.

After talking for a little while longer, the lieutenant got up to leave and started for the door when I said, "Lt. Epps, sir." He turned around and looked at me like he was waiting for me to continue. I went on to say, "Sir, you were right about it being an honor to have been chosen as one of the tank crews for the assignment, and speaking for the entire crew, we are all very proud and honored to have been chosen." The crew all shook their heads in agreement.

"Good," the lieutenant said, and then attempting to turn again, he said, "by the way, Ottley, I almost forgot, but you are up for R & R." Then he went on to tell us that a bunch of the troops had already left a few days ago, but I hadn't come off the ridge soon enough to go with them. He said that because I was late that I wouldn't have much of a choice where to go, that Tokyo and Osaka were filled up, leaving Yokohama as the only place left. I told him that I wanted to go to Tokyo, because my cousin was stationed there in the Air Force. He told me I could always catch a train from Yokohama to Tokyo, because they were only about thirty miles apart. "I guess that's where I'll go then, being I don't have any choice," I said. Then he told me to check with headquarters about going.

We were allowed to take R & R every six months, but very seldom did anyone ever get to take it on time. It is for a five-day period, meant to give you a rest and a chance to unwind from being in combat. I had been in Korea for over seven and a half months before I got the notice that I could take it. One reason was that I had been in combat most of that time. When you are on the front, there is no way you are going to get to go on R & R until you get relieved.

Right after the lieutenant left, I went to headquarters to sign up for R & R. The lieutenant was right. Yokohama was the only place left, so I told them that would have to do. They went on to tell me that I could leave for Seoul early the next day, and that I should catch my plane at the Seoul airport and not to be late. They said a jeep would take me to the airport.

They went on giving me my instructions of what to do. They told me that after I got to Yokohama, I would be taken to a checkpoint just outside of Yokohama where I would have to check my .45-caliber handgun and pistol belt, and they would hold it there until I returned. They said, "Before you leave your .45, make damn sure you remember the serial number, because you will have to repeat it back to them before getting the gun back." They also told me that I was on my own during R & R and try to stay out of trouble. Then, they gave me all the papers I needed and said have a good time.

I went back to my squad tent and told my crew that I was to leave for R & R in the morning. A jeep would be there to take me to the airport to catch my plane. I told them that I hated the idea of going alone and that I sure wish some of them were going with me, but they weren't quite eligible. I told them that there would probably be more guys from other units on the plane going to Yokohama, but it wouldn't be the same because they would be staying in Yokohama and I would be going on to Tokyo, so I would be by myself until I met my cousin.

We talked a while when Jim Blades said, "Sarg, just how much money do you have?" I told him not much, maybe twenty or so dollars. "Hell," he said, "you will want to buy souvenirs and stuff to send home, and twenty dollars isn't going to cut it. Here," he said, and handed me forty dollars.

I looked at him and said, "I don't know how or when I'll be able to pay you back."

"I'm not worried," he said, "just pay me back whenever you can."

Then I said, "Thanks a lot, Jim. It sure will help."

Forget-Me-Not
By the Disabled American Veterans

Forget-me-not; when you're lost in thought,
As you make it through the day.

Forget-me-not; I am one who fought,
And was scarred along the way.

Forget-me-not; for the freedom bought,
With the lives one can't repay.

Forget-me-not; when your child is taught,
To remember yesterday.

Forget-me-not; when the day is hot,
And you bend your knees to pray.

Forget-me-not; yes, I heard the shot,
But I did not run away.

Forget-me-not; I'm a patriot,
And I need your help today.

Photo of Hill 851, the left finger of "Heartbreak Ridge" in North Korea.
Note the tank to the left. It has been pulled down the hill to be loaded with 76 mm
ammo getting ready for the assault. The tank is SFC Dennis Ottley and crew's tank.
Their bunker, where they lived, is just up the road to the north of the tank, The bunker
shown in the lower middle of the photo is similar to Ottley and crew's bunker which is
located just over the hill shown by arrow. To the right of the photo, looking to the north
and down is the valley occupied by the Chinese Reds where the assault will take place.
(February and March, 1952)

Photos of Hill 851, the left finger of "Heartbreak Ridge" located in North Korea look-ing towards the west.

CHAPTER 23

R & R (REST AND RELAXATION)

The next morning, the jeep was there to take me to the airport to catch my plane. I couldn't believe that I was finally getting to go on R & R. Something I was eligible for about six weeks ago, but at any rate, I was glad to get my chance to see my cousin Burk Evans. He was stationed at the Tachikawa Air Force Base just west of Tokyo. He and I were really close when we were kids.

We were about an hour getting to the airport where I met other GIs that were also going on R & R, but apparently they were all going to Yokohama, and would all be staying there for their five days, while I was going on to Tokyo from Yokohama to spend my time.

When we boarded the plane, they told us that there were paper bags in the rack next to our seats just in case we felt like we were getting air sick. They didn't have to explain any more to us, except to buckle up. We knew what the bags were for as soon as they told us where they were. The seats were facing the center of the plane, so your back was against the wall.

This was the first time for me to fly in an airplane, so the first thing I did when I found my seat was grab a paper bag. I wasn't planning on getting sick, but I wanted to be ready, just in case. I made it through the entire trip without having to use the sack, but I did get a little woozy for a short time. For being my first time up in an airplane, it was not a very enjoyable trip. The plane was noisy and very uncomfortable.

After a few hours and a pretty rough ride, we finally landed at the Yokohama air strip. After getting off the plane, they directed us to a building, not too far from where we were, where we were to go to check-in.

So, we all started hoofing it across the airstrip to the building where they sent us. When we got there, they told us we had to check in our .45-caliber

206

automatic handguns along with our ammo belts. They also told us to make damn sure that we memorize the serial number off our gun, because we would be required to repeat that number back to them before they would return it to us. They continued to give us more instructions and told us we were to return to this building in five days. They gave us a time and told us not to be late, that if we were late, we would be considered AWOL (absent without leave).

All of us left to catch the bus to downtown Yokohama. After we got downtown, the rest of the guys went their way while I caught a cab to take me to the train depot. I was all alone now and felt kind of lost in a strange town. I didn't know any Japanese and I wasn't sure just how I would communicate with the natives. I got to the depot and found out that the next train to Tokyo would be early the next morning, so I went to a barber shop and got myself a haircut and a shave; the first and only time I had ever got a shave in a barber shop. It felt good.

After leaving the barber shop, I found another cab to take me to a hotel where I could get a good night's sleep. I grabbed something to eat, I went to my room, and read for a while then went to bed early. I wanted to get to the depot early. I didn't want to take any chances on missing my train.

When I got to the depot and boarded my train, I noticed that the trains appeared to be much smaller than trains in America. The tracks looked to be narrower than they were at home, but then the Japanese people also seemed smaller. When I got on the train leaving Yokohama, I couldn't believe how fast they went. We were in Tokyo before I hardly got settled. That train must have been going at least a hundred miles an hour, because it sure didn't take long to get there.

When I got off the train, I called my cousin Burk. He was stationed at the Tachikawa Air Base just out of Tokyo. He told me to meet him at a certain place in a couple hours. So, I walked around in downtown Tokyo for a while, just passing the time of day, when I came to a corner where a Japanese artist was standing with some of his drawings on display. They were all sketches of different people, mostly soldiers, which he had completed. He stopped me and asked me if I would let him do a sketch of me. I don't recall just how I communicated with him, maybe he knew enough English to get by. I don't remember how much he was going to charge me, either, but it seemed like about a dollar. Anyway, I told him 'yes' and he proceeded to sketch a portrait of me while I just stood there. After he was finished, I paid him and looked at the drawing and thought it turned out pretty damn good. It only took him a half hour or so. The size of the picture was about 10 x 15 inches. I left, thanking the artist for drawing the picture and proceeded to go to the location where Burk told me to meet him. I wanted to be early in case something happened to delay me.

Burk showed up pretty much on time, driving an air force jeep. It was great to see him. We were pretty close when we were kids, but it had been a few years since I had seen him. I asked him how he could get a jeep just to come and pick me up. He explained that with his rank, he could check out a jeep just about any time he wanted. His rank was Sr. Airman at the time, which, I believe, does consider him a non-com.

• • •

During the Korean War, around the clock planes arrived and departed in and out of the Tachikawa Air Base. A typical flight might carry 35,000 pounds of hand grenades to South Korea, returning with as many as 80 wounded GIs, arriving to be transported to the USAF hospital on the base. For thousands of servicemen whose tours took them into, through, or out of Tachikawa, the USAF hospital became the best barometer of American military activities in the Far East.

• • •

During the route to Burk's air base, he pointed out Mount Fujisan, commonly called Mt. Fuji. He told me that it was the highest mountain in Japan and it was actually a volcano, but hadn't been active for thousands of years. He also told me that about 200,000 people attempt to climb it every summer, the climbing season. I said to him, "Well, I'm not going to be here that long and probably wouldn't try it anyway."

Then he told me that he had never tried it, and didn't intend to. "Hell," he said, "I've been here for several months and I don't know of any GI that had climbed it. In the first place, you would need certain equipment to do that and I don't know of anyone who has that kind of gear." Then he told me that in the eyes of the Japanese people, "If you climb it once, you are a hero; but if you climb it a second time, they just laugh at you; then if you climb it a third time or more, you are just a damn fool and they'll just ignore you." He went on to tell me that the Japanese had a great sense of humor and would laugh at almost anything.

When we reached base, we took the jeep to the motor pool and then went to Burk's quarters. I was astonished on how he lived. I couldn't believe it. I guess I was expecting barracks like we had in the States, but he had a large room that bunked about three of them, plus they had their very own shower. I judged his quarters to be between a college dormitory and a hotel suite. I thought to myself *why didn't I join the Air Force? I never dreamed that these flyboys would have it so nice."*

Burk then brought me in a bunk to sleep on and told me I could stay there while I'm on R & R. I said, "I want to go to Tokyo and do a little shopping tomorrow. How do I get there?"

"Hell," he said, "after breakfast, we'll just check out a jeep, and I will take you to town and drop you off. You can spend all day in Tokyo, shopping and messing around all you want." And, that is exactly what he did the next three days until I caught a train back to Yokohama.

That night, Burk took me off base to a nightclub that I thought was more like a dive, because when we walked in, it was so dark and dingy, noisy, and crowded. All I could see was a bunch of GIs, mostly air force, and a few Japanese girls, some dancing. We went to a table where a few of Burk's buddies were. After introductions, he ordered us a couple of beers. I guess we were there for a couple hours, just drinking beer and talking. We talked for a while, some asked me about Korea, and how things were going there.

Burk finally spoke up and said, "Well, it's getting late and Denny's probably pretty tired and I've got to work tomorrow, so we're going to leave and go get some shut eye." I was tired and was looking to get some rest, so I stood up and told them that I was glad to meet them and then we left for the base.

The next three mornings, after breakfast, Burk checked out a jeep and took me to town. One of the first things I did was check on the best time it would be to call Sandy in Evanston. Japan's time was at least a full day's difference or more than Wyoming's time, so I wasn't sure of what time would be best to call home, but when I finally did, I had to call person to person. I wanted to make sure Sandy was home and near the phone.

I finally found a phone and made my call home. I called collect person to person, hoping my timing would be right and that Sandy would be home. She was home so we got to talk to one another for the first time in ten months. It was great to hear her voice. Letters were great, but nothing like talking to her, personally. For some reason or other, the phone company had a policy that would allow a person only three minutes to talk on the phone out of the country, but that was okay, we couldn't have afforded any more time anyway. The three minutes cost about $33, which was a lot of money in those days, especially when you didn't have it.

During the three minutes, I told her how much I missed her and asked how our son Randy was. She told me that they had a little studio apartment for which she was paying $25 a month. She said it wasn't very big, just one room with a kitchen, a hidden bed that folded up into the wall, and a bath, but it was just right for her and Randy. She told me that she was waiting tables at the Ranch Café and making pretty good tips. The Ranch Café was a restaurant in Evanston where she was working as a waitress when we got married.

During our conversation, I told her that all of us from Wyoming should be up for rotation in a month or so, but that I was thinking about staying in Korea for three more months, and that if I did, I would possibly get another promotion. Then, I told her that I was thinking about signing up again for the Army for another four years, and that I might make a career of it. She didn't take that very well. She wanted me to get my butt home and stay there.

When she told my mother what I was thinking about, my mother came unglued. Both my mother and Sandy wrote to me and told me to get home. After Paul Oaks, one of my best friends, had gotten killed in Korea, my mother was very worried about me. She was very close to Paul and wanted me home.

After three minutes of talking to Sandy, we hung up, telling each other how much we missed and loved one another. Hanging up was really hard, it made me think maybe I should get home and quit thinking about re-upping.

While I was walking around the streets of Tokyo, I ran into a studio that painted portraits off of photos. Being that I just happened to have the photos of Sandy and Randy in my wallet that I got for Christmas, I would see if they could paint portraits off of them. So, I went in and asked them if they could do it and they said they could, so I pulled the photos out of my wallet and handed them over. They looked at the photos, which were in black and white, and asked me if I wanted them in color. I asked if they could do that, and the one Japanese artist said no problem. They told me to come back in a few hours and they would have them ready for me. So, I left and proceeded down the street to the Tokyo PX (post-exchange).

The Tokyo PX was like a big department store that was controlled by the military. I believe about 90 percent of the employees were Japanese civilians. They appeared to be great workers, never stopping. The store was really busy and appeared to be a neat place to shop for souvenirs and what have you. I proceeded to look around and ended up buying a few things to send home, such as Japanese pajamas, scarves, and other souvenirs. I sent my mother and sister something also, but don't recall exactly what. The store had a section where they wrapped and labeled your gifts to send home. So, when I bought something, I would take it up to the section and have them get it ready for mailing, and then they would mail it for me.

I spent most of the three days that I had left of my R & R at the PX, buying gifts and watching the Japanese employees wrap the packages and working. It was amazing the way they wrapped the packages, so fast and so perfect. The Japanese may have been small people, but boy when they did something, it was like watching a machine because they did things so fast and so neatly. They were actually quite fun to watch. Therefore, not having much of anything else to do, I spent some of my time there at the PX just watching them.

When I left the PX that day, I stopped at the art studio to pick up the two paintings I had done. Surprisingly, they did do them in color. Each portrait was about 10 x 12 inches in size. They had painted them off of the two 2 x 4-inch black and white photos that I had left of Sandy and Randy. I personally thought they looked pretty good and told them so. I paid and thanked them for being so speedy.

I was very much surprised at how well I was communicating with the Japanese merchants. Hell, I didn't know any Japanese lingo, but they seemed to know just enough English to know what I wanted. It was a lot easier than I anticipated it to be.

While I was downtown, I went to the train depot to check out when the next train to Yokohama would be. This was my last day in Tokyo, so I thought I had better find out. There was a train leaving early the next morning, the day I had to check in at the Yokohama air base. It seemed like I would have ample time to get to Yokohama and out to the air base to catch my plane back to Korea. So, early the next morning, Burk checked out another jeep and took me to the train depot.

When I got to Yokohama, I caught the bus to the air base. I went to the building where we had checked in at on our arrival to pick up my ammo belt, pistol, and things. To get my stuff I had to tell them my name, rank, and serial number, plus the serial number on my pistol. After that, they brought my stuff to me with no problems.

All of the other GIs that had been on the same flight for R & R with me also showed up. We were all a little early for the flight, so we had to wait about an hour or so before the plane showed up.

The flight back didn't seem as bad as the flight coming. I never got a bit sick going back, although I did have a paper sack in my hands, just in case. When we landed at the Seoul airport, there was a jeep waiting to take us back to our outfits. In a way, it was kind of nice to be back with the guys, but I did want to go home. After talking to Sandy on the phone, I was even more home-sick than ever.

When I got back to our command post from R & R, the rest of the guys from Wyoming were already back. Apparently, they got back a couple days after I left. Most of them went to Tokyo, but some went to Osaka. The first thing I did, after talking to my crew and telling them how things went on R & R, was go visit Boyd Henderson and some of the others from home that I had come to Korea with. We all just kind of sat around talking to what we did while on R & R. They also indicated that they were a little disappointed that I didn't get the chance to go with them, but they all knew that I had been on Heart-break Ridge.

211

After visiting a while about our trips on R & R, we talked a little about how things were back home. Nobody seemed to have any new or different news to speak of, but they all seemed anxious to get out of Korea and go home.

Then somebody mentioned Heartbreak Ridge and wanted to know how things went. Apparently, they had heard some stories floating around the camp about it, so I tried to fill them in on just what had happened and how we did. I told them that although the main objective of the assault didn't come off as well as expected, the tank crews performed very well and my crew felt really honored to have been picked for the assignment.

The rest of the time while in reserve, was spent just training and, sometimes, we would go on a mock assault with an infantry group on a hill behind the lines. It was nice to once again get in Tank 22 (Doris) and go on these practice runs. Although these were just practice runs, we did use live ammo on them. My crew hadn't been in our tank since before we were assigned to duty on the Ridge, so it felt pretty good to get back in operation with our own tank, even if it was just practicing.

After getting back from R & R, I never went into combat again. Heartbreak Ridge would be the last of my combat experiences. The first part of May 1952, word came down that a good number of troops in the Tank Company of the 14th Infantry Regiment were up for rotation. Apparently, the GIs up for rotation had reached their quota of 37 combat points or more and were eligible to be rotated out. Most of us had beyond the quota of points needed to be eligible.

While in reserve, I talked to Lt. Epps quite a bit and told him that I was thinking about staying over in Korea for a few more months and maybe staying in the Army for another four years, but after talking to my wife I had changed my mind and would be going home. I told him that my mother got pretty upset when she heard that I was thinking about staying in Korea for a while. He agreed with me that I had best go home.

PHOTOS OF SEOUL AIRPORT (APRIL, 1952)

Curtis-Wright C-46 Commando, used for transporting troops to R and R and other destinations...

Douglas C-54 Skymaster, used to transport troops in the Far East...

Korean girls (baby-sans) looking on..

Korean kids (boy-sans) playing on the airstrip...

SR AIRMAN BURK EVANS
Stationed at Tachikawa Air Base near Tokyo, Japan
April 1952

Mount Fujisan (more commonly known as Mt. Fuji) located near Tokyo, Japan. Mt Fuji is a volcano that has been inactive for thousands of years. Approximately 200,000 climbers attempt to climb it each year durng the summer months...

Above is the portrait of Sandy, wife of SFC Dennis Ottley, that was painted by a Japanese artist while on R and R (rest and relaxation) in Tokyo. It was painted from the small photo on the right. The actual size of the painting is 10 x 12 inches, but the photo to the right is only 2 x 4 inches. (notice they painted it in color).
April 1952

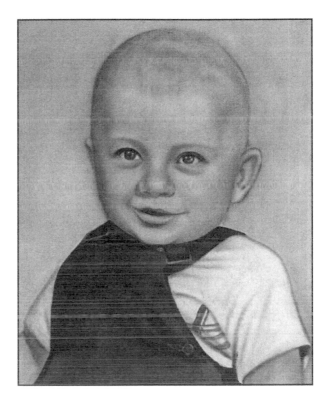

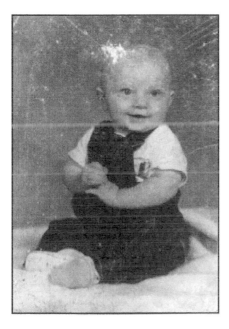

Above is the portrait of Randy, son of SFC Dennis Ottley, that was painted by a Japanese artist while on R and R (rest and relaxation) in Tokyo. It was painted from the small photo on the left. The actual size of the painting is 10 x 12 inches, but the photo to the left is only 2 x 4 inches. (notice they painted it in color).
April 1952

CHAPTER 24

MUSTERING OUT, NEXT STOP SASEBO

About the first of May, 1952, the roster came out, listing the troops that were eligible for rotation. Most all of those from Wyoming that came over together were on the list, including myself. I don't recall just how the mustering out went, but I do know that along with myself, Boyd Henderson, Ray Tanner, Jim Bateman, and Verd Erickson were on the same list and would be going home together. However, Bateman wasn't so lucky. He got appendicitis a few days before we were scheduled to leave and got sent to an Army hospital in Japan to get his appendix out. He was really disappointed.

It was about May 5, I believe, when we were scheduled to be mustered out. I believe we were about the third bunch to leave that morning. Henderson, Tanner, and Erickson were in the same bunch as I was, and we would all be going back to Wyoming together. We had all packed our duffle bags and other gear, getting ready to go. After reporting in at headquarters, we got our orders that a truck would be picking us up just outside of our quarters. The truck would then take us to the Seoul train depot where we would catch the train to Pusan.

While I was waiting, I really felt bad that I hadn't spent more time with some of my tank crew. When the mustering out roster came down, they took all of us off our regular duty so we could get ready to go. At this time, some of my crew members—Blades, Grey, and Davis—were on R & R. The only crew member left in camp was Neumann. I felt really bad that I wouldn't get to see them before I left.

I didn't even get a chance to get anyone's address. I was hoping to try to stay in contact with some of them, especially those in my tank. I wanted to make an effort after the war was over to try to make contact with some of them, but circumstances didn't work out that way. I have never been able to make contact with any of them, because I didn't have any way to find them.

Other than the Wyoming guys, I've only heard from one of my other buddies, a crew member Harvey Neumann from Missouri. He contacted me through the 25th Infantry Division Association that both of us ended up becoming a member of, but that was over fifty years after the war. We communicated and sent each other Christmas cards for several years after we made our initial contact, but we never did really get together.

So, after getting everything squared away at headquarters and getting all packed and telling all those in camp goodbye, we waited that morning for the truck to take us to the Seoul train depot. Arriving at Seoul, we had to go through a little more routine stuff before we boarded the train.

After a while, we finally boarded what looked like a rickety old train with an old coal burner for an engine. While boarding, we noticed that there were no regular seats, just wooden platforms for us to sit or lay on. There were also a lot of the windows broken out and the train was dirtier than hell. You would have thought that they could have at least cleaned the train and given us some halfway decent seats, but what the hell, we were going home and it was far better than nothing.

As we left the depot, we tried to get as comfortable as possible. We noticed as the train pulled out of the station, that the black smoke and soot coming from the engine was getting in the train through the broken windows and getting things dirtier than they already were.

We understood that the train was an old Japanese-made coal burner and would be moving along pretty slowly. We figured it was going to be several hours before we got to Pusan, so we figured we would get just as comfortable as possible and relax and listen to the train trudging down the tracks, just a rattling and clanking along at about 20 miles an hour. There wasn't much scenery to look at, just rice paddies and hills, but I believe most of us had already seen enough of the Korean scenery, so we just passed the time mostly by playing cards and reading books. We also tried to get a little sleep, but that was almost impossible. It was quite a train ride.

Several hours later, we arrived at Pusan. I'm not sure how long we were there, but I don't believe we were there long. Maybe long enough to eat and shower. Also, I believe we had to turn in our .45-caliber pistols and belts at Pusan. After roll call and checking things out, they loaded us on some kind of a ferry boat on an overnight trip, taking us across the Korean Strait to Sasebo, Japan, where we would spend three or four days going through more inspections and more processing.

When war broke out in Korea, Sasebo became the main launching point for the United Nations and the United States Forces. Millions of tons of ammunitions, fuel tanks, trucks, and supplies flowed through Sasebo on their way to UN forces in Korea. The number of military personnel stationed there grew to about 20,000. It was also used for moving American troops in and out of the Far East.

While in Sasebo, we, meaning myself, Henderson, Tanner, and Erickson, got to go off base one time to go to a movie. I don't recall the name of the movie, but I remember it was great to be able to get out and finally, at least, go to movie. The rest of the time, except for inspections, we just laid around reading and writing letters, except we had to pull duty once in a while over some kind of detail or other.

I remember that while in Sasebo, we went through a lot of different types of inspections. The first inspection we went through just after we go there was to completely empty our duffle bags and other gear to show that we didn't have any souvenirs or objects from the war that we weren't supposed to have. We also had the "short arm" inspection and the "spread your cheeks" inspection, and went through lines a couple times, getting different shots in the arm by some damn needle.

We had been in Sasebo about three days when we got the word that we would be shipping out the next morning. We had to get up pretty early that morning, eat breakfast, fall in formation, and go through roll call once again before loading up on trucks to take us to the docks. It seemed like every time we got somewhere or left somewhere, they would have to take roll call. I guess it was to make sure no one had gone AWOL or was missing.

Arriving that morning at the docks with all our gear, we left the trucks and fell into formation for roll call, once again. As they called our name, we were to board the ship and then someone would direct us to our quarters, which were, once again, a compartment full of bunks about four bunks deep.

There, we were, once again, all crammed in like a bunch of sardines in a compartment full of bunks, but then we were going home, so it didn't matter. In boarding the ship, I was separated from my Wyoming buddies, but, once again, it didn't take long to locate them.

This ship was named the *USNS Private Joe P. Martinez*, who was a Medal of Honor recipient during WWII. Martinez was from Colorado and was the first Hispanic/American soldier to receive the MOH. He was also the first to receive it for combat heroism during the invasion of Pearl Harbor.

The Martinez was smaller than the *USNS Gen. Weigel*, the ship we came over to Korea on. While the *Weigel* could hold approximately 5,000 troops, the *Martinez* could only hold about 4,000, but the *Martinez* was a faster ship.

After leaving the Sasebo port, we were told that we would be going back to the States by way of Honolulu. They said that we would have a layover while there and we would be able to leave the ship for about five hours.

Amazingly, I did not get sea sick the entire trip back to the States. I don't know why, because we had a pretty rough ride from Japan to Hawaii. We had bad weather all the way to Honolulu. It rained all the way with high winds, causing high waves and rough water. You couldn't stay up on deck very long; it was raining so hard most of the time. So, the first few days were not much fun.

After four or five days of rough going and bad weather, we finally reached Honolulu. I believe we were all damn glad to have a chance to dock and spend a few hours on shore. Plus, we were all kind of looking forward to seeing Hawaii.

Before we left the ship, they told us that we only had five hours and that we better be back on time because they would wait for no one and you would be counted AWOL. They also told us that if you were not 21 years of age, do not try to get in the bars. They said the Hawaiian cops were big Hawaiian men and that they would not stand for any nonsense. So, they said their advice to us was stay sober and out of trouble.

Some of the troops didn't listen very well; some did end up in jail, and some ended up being carried on the ship by someone helping them or on stretchers, plus some also ended up in the hospital, all from having confrontations with the cops. Those troops in jail and the hospital didn't make it to the States on that trip. Hawaii was still a territory at the time, and didn't have much tolerance with American soldiers getting rowdy or drunk. Their cops had some pretty big sticks that they carried for any nonsense and they didn't hesitate to use them.

As we left the ship, we were greeted by Hawaiian girls with an "Aloha" greeting and a "*lei*" was put over our heads. After we left the ship, we just wandered the streets, bought a few souvenirs, and had a few snacks. I bought Sandy an authentic grass skirt, plus something for Randy and my mother. Erickson and I were still too young to get in the bars so none of us did any drinking. Henderson and Tanner were plenty old enough, but they just stayed with us.

I was quite disappointed with the area of Hawaii we were in. It appeared to be kind of dirty and low class. We didn't get very far from the docks. The street we were on just had a bunch of small side stores where you could get a snack, buy souvenirs, get tattoos, or have your picture taken with some Hawaiian girl in a bathing suit. One of the girls did try to talk us into one of the stores, wanting us to have our picture taken with her, but nobody would do it and we just shunned her and kept walking. We weren't about to spend our money for something like that.

A Soldier's Prayer
A Poem from the Album of Edwin Laub, 1932

Now I lay me down to sleep, I pray the Lord my soul to keep;
Grant no other soldier to take, my shoes and socks before I wake.
Try and guard me in my sleep, and keep my bunk upon its feet,
And in the morning let me wake, breathing whiffs of sirloin steak.
Please protect me in my dreams, and make it better than it seems.
Grant the time may swiftly fly, when I myself may rest "or try"
In a snowy feather bed, with a pillow beneath my head.
Far away from all these scenes, from the smell of hash and beans,
Oh, treat me to some ham and eggs, or a stack of mother's hotcakes.
Thou who knowest all my woes, feed me in my dingy throes,
Take me back and I promise thee, never more to cross the sea.

•   •   •

"One man with courage makes a majority." – Andrew Jackson

The USNS Pvt. Joe P. Martinez

This ship was named after Martinez for heroism on December 7, 1941, during the invasion of Pearl Harbor. He was the first Hispanic/American to receive the Congressional Medal of Honor during WWII.

CHAPTER 25

FORT LAWTON, CAMP CARSON, AND THEN HOME

We were now leaving Honolulu on the same ship, the *Martinez*, all hoping to have better and smoother sailing. They told us that we would reach Seattle in about nine or ten days and from there, we would be going to Fort Lawton just out of Seattle for mustering out and more processing.

We were now back on the ship ready to leave Hawaii, only this time, the weather looked good and indicated that we may have a much smoother trip the rest of the way to the States. So, to pass the time, we spent most of our time up on deck, once again watching the fish, the birds, and the wake. It was quite a sight to see the fish feed off the garbage left by the ship. The trip from Honolulu to Seattle did turn out to be pretty nice. We had good weather all the way.

We entered the bay called the Puget Sound that took us in to Seattle, WA, about May 20, 1952. We had been on the water for 14 days, leaving Sasebo, Japan. As we neared Seattle, looking over across the bay toward Canada and the surrounding area, I thought it was some of the most beautiful country I had ever seen. I said to my buddies, "Isn't that beautiful country, a big difference from the scenery we had in Korea." Then I added, "But then, Korea had been battered all to hell, so I guess it wouldn't be fair to compare." They all agreed. We were all anxious to get our feet on good old American soil, but before we left the ship, we had to make sure everything was ship shape, and that took a while.

As we disembarked from the ship, we got a grandstand welcome from the crowd on the docks. At the end of the ramp, the Red Cross was there handing out coffee and donuts. It was a nice greeting, and all the troops seemed to be impressed by it. The donuts tasted great, especially after eating the chow on the ship. But, the chow on this ship was much better than the chow was on the *Weigel* going over.

227

After leaving the ship, we all got back in formation for roll call and then they loaded us in trucks and took us to a fort called Lawton. When arriving at the fort, they directed us to our barracks, where we would be staying for the next few days, and then told us that as soon as we got settled, it wouldn't be too long before chow would be ready.

Fort Lawton was the second largest port of embarkation of soldiers and materials to the Far East during WWII and the Korean War. It was located in the City of Seattle, but was officially closed in the year of 2011. It was named after Maj. Gen. Henry Ware Lawton.

While we were at Lawton, about all we did was go through more lines for more inspections and processing. We all just stayed on base. Although, we could have got a pass to go to downtown Seattle for a movie or something, we just decided to stay on base and get a good rest.

The worst thing that happened to us while we were at Lawton, as far as I was concerned, was going through the "de-lousing chamber." It was a shack where you had to be completely naked. They had you go through it to make sure you got rid of any lice or fleas that you may have picked up while overseas. Going through the chamber, the haze was so thick it was hard to keep your eyes open. Even if you could have kept your eyes open, you wouldn't have been able see much of anything. It was bad.

After a few days at Lawton, that afternoon they trucked us to the train depot and put us on a train to Camp Carson (now known as Fort Carson), CO. We took the train through northern Washington to Billings, MT, and then south through Wyoming to Colorado. A good share of the trip was at night-time, so we didn't get to see much, but the scenery was beautiful through Washington and Montana before it got dark.

We arrived in Colorado Springs, CO, about May 24, where we boarded some trucks that took us on into the camp. They took us to the barracks where we would be quartered for the next few days until discharge.

We had a few days to relax and prepare ourselves for going home. All of us—Henderson, Tanner, Erickson, and I—would be getting discharged from the Army at this time. We all received our mustering out pay of $300 each, so we had some money to get home on. We got together and tried to decide on whether we wanted to fly home or take the train out of Denver. So, we went to Denver to check out things and take in a movie. While there, we decided to take the plane and fly into Salt Lake City, so we went to the airport and bought our plane tickets.

Before we left Camp Carson, the four of us decided to tear a one-dollar bill in four pieces with each of us taking a piece of the dollar, with a promise that the next time we all got together, we would tape the dollar bill back together and buy us each a beer. Back in those days, beer was only ten cents a glass or twenty to twenty-five cents a bottle, so the one-dollar bill would have been enough to buy the four beers. However, it never happened, because we just never got back together again. The only one that I saw much of was Boyd. I saw Ray a couple times, but I never did see Verd again

On our final day as soldiers in the Army, we were ready to go home, so we took a bus out of Camp Carson to Denver. When we got to the airport, we got bad news; we found out that our flight would be hours late and there would be a big delay. Boy, what a mistake, we should have taken the train, but it was too late to change our minds, so we waited.

We could have taken the train a hell of a lot cheaper, and probably would have got into Evanston sooner, plus Sandy wouldn't have had to worry about finding someone to take her down to the Salt Lake airport, but we decided to stay with the plane. We had already bought tickets.

Sandy didn't have a car and didn't know how to drive at the time, so she asked a couple of our friends if they would take her down in one of their cars. Harvey Johnston agreed to take his car. When we got to Salt Lake my wife, Sandy, with our son Randy were there to greet me, along with Harvey and Vince Caldwell. Both had been in the Army with me at Camp Campbell, but neither ever went overseas.

Boyd Henderson's wife, Beverly, came down with his folks to greet him and pick him up, Ray Tanner's wife and kids came down from Mt. View, WY, to get him; and Verd Erickson's family from Afton, WY, came to pick him up.

Also, my folks, who were living in Murray, UT, at the time, were there to greet me. It was great to see everyone and great to be going home. Now being discharged from the Army, I would have a chance to spend time with my family and see my son grow up.

We got home on May 29, just a few days before Sandy's and Randy's birthdays. Sandy's birthday would be on June 4, and Randy's on June 3. Randy was born just four hours before his mother's birthday. He was just starting to walk when I got home. He was a little wobbly, but it was neat watching him.

Sandy had been living in a recently-built, small apartment complex with four studio-type units located right across the street from our old high school. The apartment had one big room as the living room and bedroom, a small kitchen separate from the living room, and a bathroom. The bed folded up into the wall when it wasn't in use, so the room wasn't so crowded in the daytime. It was a cute little apartment and suited us just fine for the time being. She was paying $25 per month, including the utilities.

From the time I got home, I started calling Sandy "Honey-bucket." I don't know why, but I guess I just thought it was kind of cute. I called her that for several months until one of my "good" buddies told her what it meant in Korea (a bucket full of human waste). She took it pretty well, except she gave me a poke and called me a "smart ass," but then we just laughed at it.

One of the first things we did when I got home was to take time to go visit her folks, my sister and her family, and my brothers. Then I started looking for a job. I found one immediately at the same place I was working at when I went in the army. It was at the East End Texaco as a service station attendant and gas jockey, but it was now under different ownership. Two brothers, Preston and Fay Eyre, had just recently purchased it from Bill Kitchen, my old boss. I went to work for them immediately.

At that time, Sandy was working as a waitress at the Ranch Café. We didn't make much money, but it was a living. We weren't too worried about what the pay was, we were more worried about just being able to get a job and being able to pay our bills and buy groceries.

When all of us Korean War veterans came home, we just went out and found a job and went to work, just as if we had never been gone. All our family and friends seemed to have been glad to see us and happy that we were back, but nobody asked us any questions about where we had been or how the war was going, and we didn't talk about it, either. Hell, even if we had, they probably wouldn't have known where Korea was or that a war was even going on. After all, they called it "the Forgotten War."

"Forgotten War?" It's been over 60 years since I got home from Korea, and I don't think there is a Korean War veteran that will ever forget the hot miserable summers, the cold sub-zero winters, or the damn big hills that they had to climb, fortify, and defend. I know I never will.

•　•　•

We Will Never Forget….
by Jack Hegarty

Fought in the fifties and forgotten since those times.
The Korean War in history books is given few lines.

But to they who served and to they who lost kin,
It is never forgotten and the memories do not dim.

We went willingly along with our friends,
Not knowing what waited or where it would end.

Some did not return from the hills over there.
It is they we wish to honor and to keep in our prayers.

They will be forever young as they were when they fell,
Never to grow old with war stories to tell.

In the blazing heat and bitter cold of the night,
Through mountains and valleys they carried the fight.

Their honor and glory shines brighter each day,
And we ask you to remember them with us today.

• • •

"Some people give time, some give money, some their skills and connections, some literally give their life's blood. But everyone has something to give." — Barbara Bush

• • •

"In the future days, which we seek to make secure, we look forward to a world founded upon four essential human freedoms.

The first is freedom of speech and expression—everywhere in the world.

The second is freedom of every person to worship GOD in his own way—everywhere in the world.

The Third is freedom from want—everywhere in the world.

The Fourth is freedom from fear—everywhere in the world.

The world order which we seek is the cooperation of free countries, working together in a friendly, civilized society. The nation has placed its destiny in the hands, heads, and hearts of its millions of free men and women, and its faith in freedom under the guidance of God. Freedom means the supremacy of human rights everywhere. Our support goes to those who struggle to gain those rights and keep them. Our strength is our unity of purpose. To that high concept, there can be no end save victory."
— Franklin Delano Roosevelt

• • •

AFTER THOUGHTS

This story was written by memory only. All persons, events, and happenings mentioned in this story are real and true, as I remember them. However, there may be some mistakes such as names spelled wrong, some ranks may not be accurate, plus some events may be off a little on the time and dates. I apologize for any misgivings that may offend anyone, but I thank you for reading the book and hope you enjoyed it.

·   ·   ·

The Korean War was a bloody, brutal, physical war, fought largely on the ground over some of the most unfriendly terrain imaginable in temperatures that ranged from 100 degrees plus in the summer, to as much as 50 degrees below zero in the winter. Our military, on the ground and in the air, were instrumental in pounding an estimate of 1,500,000+ casualties on the Chinese and North Korean troops during the conflict.

The Korean War was considered, by many, as deadly for the United States as World War I was. They believed that the two wars were very similar in the way they were fought, where you had trench raids back and forth, especially during the last two years of the conflict, as in WWI, where the armies fought from opposing trench lines. Hand-to-hand combat was common. There were a lot of casualties.

A total of 5,720,000 Americans served in the Korean War. Over 33,000 lost their lives, over 7,200 became POWs (prisoners of war), and over 7,000 still remain missing. It was a war where a total of 21 countries finally ended up joining together to defend the people of South Korea from annihilation and tyranny of the Soviet Union backed armies of the communist countries of North Korea and Red China.

Because of the United States and the United Nations involvement in the war, the communist movement was dealt a death blow, and now many who lived under communism are free. No, freedom is indeed not free, but that is not true in North Korea where, to this day, there is no freedom at all.

Was the Korean War worth it? Why should it be remembered? These are the big questions asked by many over the years. My suggestion is to research the pros and cons, the whys and wherefores, and create your own opinion, based on what you find.

. . .

Korean War veterans protected South Korea from totalitarian communism and prevented it from spreading to the rest of the world. The citizens of the United States should be proud of those veterans that served during the Korean War. They should thank them for a job well done by ending the North Korean communist aggression. Nobody realized that it was the opening of the Cold War that would be going on until 1989. Today, South Korea is in the first rank of nations due to the sacrifices made by the veterans of this war, and to this day, maintains a thriving economy.

. . .

Carved in stone on the Korean War Veterans Memorial in Washington, DC, are these words:
OUR NATION HONORS ITS SONS AND DAUGHTERS WHO ANSWERED THE CALL
TO DEFEND A COUNTRY THEY NEVER KNEW AND A PEO-PLE THEY NEVER MET.

. . .

Some say the war was not in vain, and should not be forgotten. It should be considered victorious, because although the war ended in an armistice, it was successful in stopping the communist movement.

No matter how personal their beliefs were about the war, almost every one that served time in Korea felt it was their duty to go. At that time, communism appeared to be getting somewhat popular within the boundaries of the United States and growing throughout the world. So, most veterans that served during that time were anxious to help stop that movement in any way they could.

· · ·

Donald Knox in his book titled, *The Korean War* wrote: "To most Americans, Korea is a forgotten war. To many, it was unreal. Ordinary lives were unruffled by the distant echoes of battle. The home front made no sacrifices. If neither one's friends nor one's family were directly involved, the war could have been fought on Mars."

· · ·

Unlike World War II, the folks never had to worry about shortages on food supplies such as sugar, flour, and butter, etc. They never had to worry about ration stamps. They never had to worry about the shortage of rubber or other materials, and they didn't have to worry about gasoline being rationed. Plus, paper drives and scrap metal drives were no longer needed, and US saving bonds and saving stamps were no longer being pushed for folks to buy.

· · ·

The author of *The Coldest Winter*, David Halberstam, wrote in his book about the Korean War veteran that: "So many of them had for so long kept it inside themselves. No one wanted to hear about the war when they had first come home, so they never talked about it, not to their families or to their oldest friends. Or when they did, no one understood—or worse, wanted to understand. Their children would most often grow up knowing only that their fathers served in the war, but almost nothing else. They would complain to their fathers, that they were never willing to talk about the war. They mourned those who had not come back, but they shared it with only one another."

· · ·

It was a long time after my four sons grew up, old enough to understand what I was talking about, before I started talking about my experiences in Korea. I felt like they should know and that they had a right to know. I was very proud of my performance in Korea. I never considered myself as a hero, but I served my country honorably. Whether right or wrong, I have always been proud to be able to say, "I've done my part. I served my country proudly, and I will never regret my time spent there."

It's been over 60 years since I returned from the Korean War, but not long enough to make me forget. I can still see some of the happenings of the war. I can still remember the cold, cold winters and watching our troops tromp up those hills in snow knee deep, dodging enemy fire. I can still remember standing up in those cold tanks, guarding our position; I can still hear the artillery shells whistling over our heads coming from the north; plus, I can still remember eating those damn C-rations a good share of the time. Yeah, there are some things that are burned into a guy's memory so much that you can never forget, even though there are some a guy wishes he could.

No, as far as I'm concerned, like many other veterans, the Korean War has not been forgotten! Certainly not by those that served in the war, or the families and friends whose loved ones were KIA (killed in action) or are still listed as MIA (missing in action). There are still over 7,000 American troops listed as MIA at this time. There are families who are still waiting for closure. Let's hope and pray that someday they find enough information on their loved ones that are still missing to be able to accept closure.

•   •   •

AMERICA is a land filled with courageous, giving people.
People who fight for what is right.
People who do not tolerate bullies.
People who are there in times of crisis,
And people who lend a hand.
BE PROUD TO CALL YOURSELF AN AMERICA,
(Author Unknown)

South Korea, "The Land of the Morning Calm." A group of words that began in the fourteenth century was the interpretation of Korea by the English, at that time. Centuries later, the nickname was coined by Percival Lowell, author of, *Chosen, the Land of the Morning Calm*, written in 1885. The descriptive name has been with South Korea ever since. It may once have been a fitting nickname for the country, but I know of about three years that the mornings weren't so calm.

South Korea, now officially called "The Republic of Korea," today has become one of Asia's top major industrial countries with the fourth largest economy. It now has a population of over 50 million. Seoul, now one of the largest cities in the world, has a population of over 10 million. South Korea became a member of the United Nations in 1991.

Was it worth it? You decide!

• • •

"Let every nation know, whether it wishes us well or ill, we shall pay any price, bear any burden, meet any hardship, support any friend, oppose any foe, TO ASSURE THE SURVIVAL AND SUCCESS OF LIBERTY." —John F. Kennedy

• • •

Freedom Is Not Free
By Trudy (Wife of a Korean War Vet)

We enjoy this country's freedom from sea to shining sea,
And that precious freedom was bought for you and me.
It was bought by every serviceman who heard his country's call,
And was willing to make the sacrifice if it be great or small.
God bless the servicemen at home and over the sea,
And tell them that we all know that Freedom Is Not Free!
We pledge allegiance to this land, this land of the free and the brave,
And our hearts begin to swell as we see "Old Glory" wave.
Tears begin to fall for them who died for liberty.
They made the supreme sacrifice to keep this country free.
God bless the servicemen at home and over the sea,
And tell them that we all know that Freedom Is Not Free!

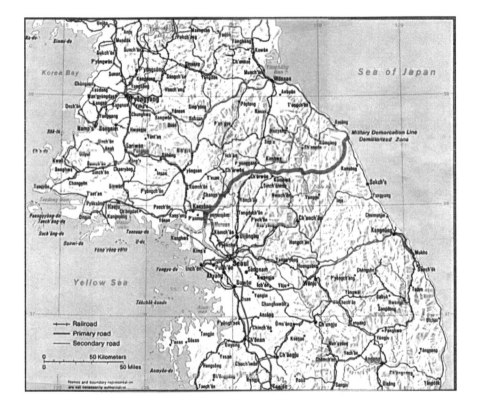

The President of the Republic of Korea

June 1, 2010

Dennis J. Ottley
150 Fox Point Loop Road
Evanston WY 82930-4784

Dear Dennis J. Ottley,

This year as we commemorate the sixtieth anniversary of the outbreak of the Korean War, we honor your selfless sacrifice in fighting tyranny and aggression. We salute your courage in enduring the unimaginable horrors of war. We pay tribute to your commitment in protecting liberty and freedom.

We Koreans made a promise to build a strong and prosperous country that upholds peace and freedom so that the sacrifices that you made would not have been in vain. We have faithfully kept that promise. Korea today is a vibrant democracy with a robust economy and we are actively promoting peace and stability around the world. Korea transformed itself from a country of received aid to one that provides aid to others. We are proud of what we managed to accomplish and we wish to dedicate these achievements to you.

The Korean government has been inviting Korean War veterans every year as part of its Revisit Korea Program since 1975. This year we will be inviting 2,400 Korean War veterans and their families. We Koreans and myself in particular look forward to welcoming you. We hope that you will see what you made possible and hope that your families will feel renewed pride in what you did for us many years ago.

Please accept, once again, our warmest gratitude and deepest respect. You will always remain our true Heroes and we assure you that we will continue to do our best to make you proud. On behalf of the Korean people, I would like to say "Thank you."

Sincerely yours,

Lee Myung-bak
President, Republic of Korea

CPSIA information can be obtained
at www.ICGtesting.com
Printed in the USA
LVOW05s0830290317
528836LV00034B/688/P